Hazards

Garrett Nagle

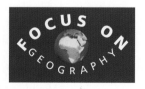

FOCUS ON GEOGRAPHY

Yeovil College

Contents

Chapter 1
Environmental hazards

Environmental hazards are eye-catching. Sudden, intense hazards such as volcanic eruptions, gas explosions, and earthquakes grip people's attention and help to sell newspapers. By contrast, other long-term hazards, such as drought, can pass by almost unnoticed, especially in countries where drought is rare. In addition, there is a great deal of confusion regarding hazards, partly because we recall the ones we see on the television and read about in the press. Unfortunately, the reporting is not always accurate and reports tend to provide instant dramatic descriptions, often when details are far from clear. Therefore, it is important to consider some of the older case studies which allow for evaluation and reflection.

In this chapter we discuss the definition of a hazard and a disaster; we examine types of hazards, trends in environmental hazards, and the geographic features of hazards. These include the people at risk, the areas at risk, and the attempts to reduce the risk of hazards and disasters.

Following the introduction in this chapter, chapters 2 to 4 deal largely with tectonic hazards, while chapters 4 to 8 examine climatological-geomorphological hazards. Chapters 9 to 13 investigate human-induced hazards. The chapters show that people are not bystanders who are unable to influence the environment; human activity can do much to create and/or intensify the risk of environmental hazards.

WHAT ARE HAZARDS AND DISASTERS?

'A hazard is a perceived natural event which has the potential to threaten both life and property – a disaster is the realisation of this hazard' (Whittow, 1980). A distinction can therefore be made between extreme events in nature which are *not* environmental hazards (because people and/or property are not at risk) and environmental hazards in which people and/or property *are* at risk.

Environmental hazards are caused by people's use of dangerous environments (Figure 1.1). To a large extent, environmental hazards are caused by human behaviour, namely the failure to recognise the potential hazard and act accordingly. The term 'natural hazard' is not a precise description, as hazards are not just the result of 'natural' events.

The term 'environmental hazard' includes both natural and human hazards. It suggests a range of hazards from natural to man-made, local to global, and subtle to intense. Some hazards are voluntary, such as smoking, whereas

Figure 1.1 *People at risk of hazards – flooding in Dhaka, Bangladesh*

others are involuntary, such as *tsunami* (large waves). Some, such as drought, are difficult to define because there may be some confusion with other factors such as malnutrition and seasonal hunger.

One of the most widely used classifications of natural hazards is shown in Figure 1.2. This divides hazards into geophysical (climatological, meteorological, geological and geomorphological) and biological (floral and faunal). Most hazard research has focused upon geophysical hazards, and they are certainly more eye-catching than biological hazards. On the other hand, biological hazards such as bacterial and viral diseases, kill more people each year. As the table suggests, almost anything can be considered a hazard if it puts people's lives and livelihoods at risk.

Environmental hazards have a number of common characteristics:

- the origin of the hazard is clear and produces distinct effects, such as flooding causing death by drowning
- the warning time is short (although drought is an exception)
- most losses to life and property occur shortly after the environmental hazard – these are often related to secondary hazards such as fire and contaminated water
- in some areas, especially in economically less developed countries (ELDCs), the risk of exposure is largely involuntary – normally due to people forced to live in hazardous areas; by contrast, in most economically more developed

Geophysical		Biological	
Climate and meteorological	**Geological and geomorphological**	**Floral**	**Faunal**
Snow and ice Droughts Floods Frosts Hail Heatwaves Tropical cyclones Tornadoes	Avalanches Earthquakes Erosion, e.g. soil erosion and coastal erosion Landslides Shifting sand Tsunami Volcanic eruptions	Fungal diseases, e.g. athlete's foot, Dutch elm disease, wheat stem rust Infestations, e.g. weeds, water hyacinth Hay fever Poisonous plants	Bacterial and viral diseases, e.g. influenza, malaria, smallpox, rabies Infestations, e.g. rabbits, termites, locusts Lightning and fires Venomous animal bites

Figure 1.2 *Classification of natural hazards by main causal agents*
Source: Burton, I. and Kates, R., 1964, The perception of natural hazards in resource management, Natural resources journal, 3, 412-21

countries (EMDCs) people occupy hazard areas as much through choice as through ignorance or necessity

- the disaster occurs with a scale and intensity that requires emergency response.

It is possible to characterise hazards and disasters in a number of ways:

1 **Magnitude** – the size of the event, e.g. Force 10 on the Beaufort Scale for wind speed, the maximum height or discharge of a flood, or the size of an earthquake on the Richter Scale

2 **Frequency** – how often an event of a certain size occurs. For example, a flood of one metre in height may occur, on average, every year on a particular river, while a flood of two metres in height might occur only every ten years. The frequency is sometimes called the recurrence interval

3 **Duration** – the length of time that the environmental hazard exists. This varies from a matter of hours (urban smog), to decades (drought)

4 **Areal extent** – the size of the area covered by the hazard. It can range from very small-scale (an avalanche chute), to continental (drought)

5 **Spatial concentration** – is the distribution of hazards over space. For example, where they are concentrated in certain areas, such as tectonic plate boundaries, coastal locations, valleys

6 **Speed of onset** – this is rather like the 'time-lag' in a flood hydrograph. It is the time difference between the start of the event and the peak of the event. It varies from rapid events, such as the Kobe earthquake, to slow events, such as drought in the Sahel of Africa

7 **Regularity** – some hazards are regular (cyclones) whereas others are much more random (earthquakes and volcanoes).

Some of these can be shown be shown on a hazard event profile (Figure 1.3).

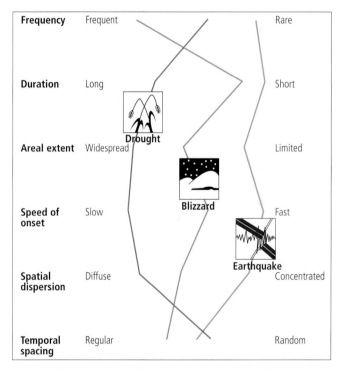

Figure 1.3 *Hazard event profiles for characteristic drought, blizzard and earthquake*
Source: Burton, I. Kates, R. and White, G., 1993, The environment as hazard, Guildford Press

QUESTIONS

1 Study Figure 1.3 which shows hazard event profiles for droughts, blizzards and earthquakes.

a) Compare and contrast earthquakes and droughts as shown in Figure 1.3.

b) One measurement of an environmental hazard has been left out of the diagram. Which one? Suggest reasons why it has been left out.

c) Make a copy of Figure 1.3 and draw the environmental hazard profile for any two of the following: tropical cyclone, landslide, volcano, river flood, smog.

THE GLOBAL PATTERN OF HAZARDS

Disasters which have killed over 500 000 people this century include drought in India (1900) and the former USSR (1921), and floods in China (1928, 1931, 1939). Since World War II there have been other massive killers – the Bengal cyclone (1970), the earthquake at Tanshen, China (1976), and drought in Mozambique (1981) and Ethiopia (1984).

About 90% of the world's environmental hazards which cause more than one hundred deaths in a single event are caused by four types of hazard:

- floods – 40% of deaths
- tropical storms – 20%
- earthquakes – 15%
- drought – 15%.

Figure 1.4 shows the impact of selected hazards on the number of deaths, the number of people affected and substantial economic damage, (defined as more than 1% of annual gross national product (GNP)). However, it is difficult to be precise about drought in terms of its extent, duration, impact and damage. By contrast, the data for earthquakes is quite reliable because they are easy to detect and monitor. The main areas subject to tropical storms, earthquakes, tornadoes and volcanic activity are shown in Figure 1.5.

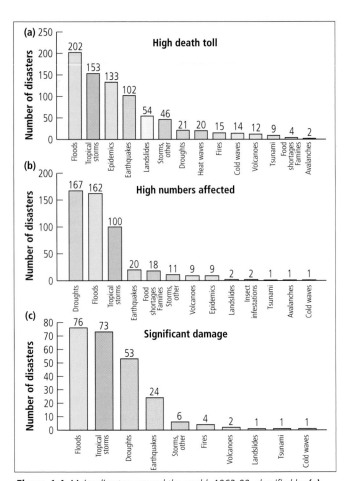

Figure 1.4 Major disasters around the world, 1963-92, classified by **(a)** high death toll (over 100 deaths), **(b)** high numbers affected (over 1% of the population), **(c)** substantial economic damage (losses of over 1% of GNP)
Source: Hewitt, K., 1997, Regions of risk: a geographical introduction to disasters, Longman

Figure 1.5 Areas at high risk from some natural hazards
Source: adapted, in part, from Wijkman, A. and Timberlake, L., 1984, Natural disasters: Acts of God or acts of Man, Earthscan

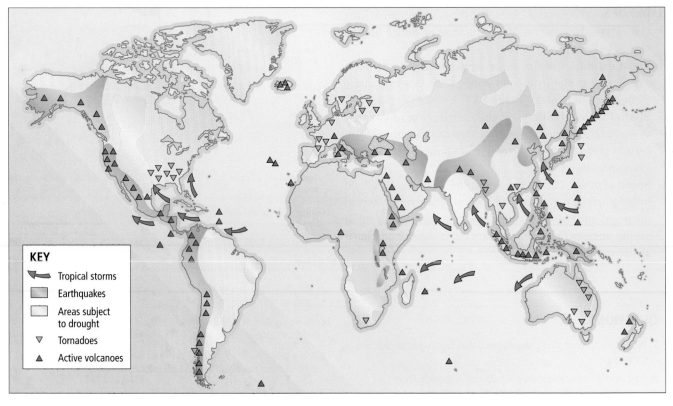

KEY
- Tropical storms
- Earthquakes
- Areas subject to drought
- Tornadoes
- Active volcanoes

Hazards affect EMDCs and ELDCs in different ways. Between 1947 and 1980, 85% of all lives lost through natural disaster were in Asia, 4% in the Caribbean and central America, and 4% in South America (Figure 1.6). By contrast, Europe and Africa accounted for 2% each, North America 1%, and Australia just 0.3%. These figures exclude the former USSR and lives lost due to drought. During Hurricane Agnes in the USA in 1972, 250 000 people were evacuated but only a dozen people died. By contrast, in Bangladesh in 1970 over 225 000 people were killed in one tropical cyclone. As Figure 1.6 shows, the biggest loss of life is in developing countries. To be poor is to be vulnerable.

Continental area	Lives lost (no.)	Disaster events (no.)	Average loss of life per event
North America	11 531	358	32
Central America and the Caribbean	50 676	80	633
South America	49 265	75	657
Europe	26 694	119	224
Africa	25 540	34	751
Asia	1 054 090	437	2412
Australasia	4502	16	282
Total	1 222 298	1119	1092

Figure 1.6 *Natural disasters 1947-80*
Source: Hewitt, K., 1997, Regions of risk: a geographical introduction to disasters, Longman

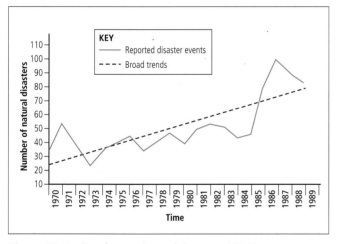
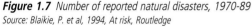

Figure 1.7 *Number of reported natural disasters, 1970-89*
Source: Blaikie, P. et al, 1994, At risk, Routledge

QUESTIONS

1 Describe the areas at risk from drought and earthquakes as shown in Figure 1.5. How do you account for these different distributions?

2 Give contrasting reasons why there are no data available in Figure 1.6 for **(i)** lives lost in the former USSR and **(ii)** lives lost due to drought.

3 Study Figure 1.7 which shows the number of natural disasters, 1970-89. Briefly describe the trend in disasters during this period. Give reasons to explain the trend in reported disasters.

THE CHANGING IMPACT OF DISASTERS

There is some evidence that the death rate from natural hazards and disasters is increasing (Figure 1.8). This is due to population growth, economic growth, increasing use of hazardous environments, and more hazards and disasters. There is also increased awareness of risks and environments at risk. In addition, when there are fewer wars or economic recession (which usually dominate the press) other world events such as hazards are reported.

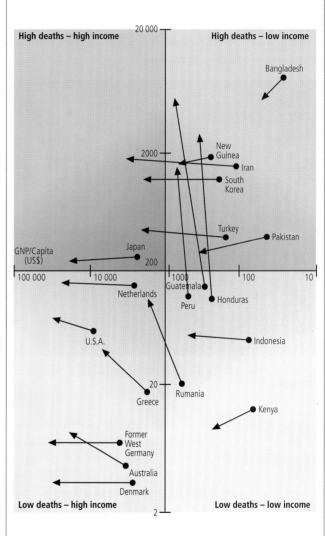

Figure 1.8 *Relationship between deaths from natural hazards per million people and national income levels for selected countries, 1973-86*
Source: Burton, I., Kates, R. and White, G., 1993, The environment as hazard, Guildford Press

In the 1970s and 1980s about three million people were killed by environmental hazards, and a further 820 million people were affected by them. It has been calculated that environmental hazards cost the global economy at least US$40 billion in losses and US$15 billion in relief and rehabilitation.

The loss to life and property experienced in a disaster is affected by a number of factors:

- size of hazard
- population density
- level of adjustment to hazard
- experience of previous hazards
- perception of hazard threat.

Environmental hazards claim more lives in poorer countries. Over 90% of deaths related to environmental hazards occur in developing countries (Figure 1.9). For example, tropical cyclones in Asia cause more deaths in poorer countries compared with wealthier countries. This is partly because poorer countries cannot afford disaster planning procedures or effective prevention methods.

Figure 1.9 *The impact of a disaster in a developing country – flood victims in Bangladesh*

In developing countries, environmental hazards are causing an increase in the number of deaths as well as in economic costs. The increase in the number of deaths is due to a number of factors:

- population growth and the use of marginal (unsafe) land for dwellings
- a shortage of land due to environmental deterioration
- economic growth creating new hazards such as chemical spills and radiation leaks
- technical innovations such as high rise flats and large dams.

In general, the impact of environmental hazards in developed countries has a greater economic cost but causes fewer deaths – 75% of the economic damage occurs in developed countries (Figure 1.10).

Figure 1.10 *The impact of a disaster in a developed country – hurricane damage in Florida*

QUESTIONS

1 Study Figure 1.8.

a) Describe the trends

b) Briefly give **two** contrasting reasons to explain the trend that you have described.

2 Study Figure 1.8 which shows the number of deaths per million people and national income levels.

a) Which developed country is among the high deaths category?

b) Which newly industrialising country is among the high deaths category?

c) Which less developed country is among the low deaths category?

d) Which countries have shown the highest increase in the death rate? Suggest **two** contrasting reasons which could explain the rise in the death rate.

e) Which countries have shown the greatest reductions in the death rate? Suggest **two** contrasting reasons which could explain the reduction in the death rate.

WHAT CAUSES ENVIRONMENTAL HAZARDS?

Environmental hazards become disasters when people and property are affected by such events. Although the cause of the hazard may be geophysical or biological this is only part of the explanation. It is because people live in hazardous areas that hazards occur. So why do they live in such places? The **behavioural** school of thought considers that environmental hazards are the result of natural events. For example, in some developing areas, shanty towns are built on steep slopes or very close to areas which flood regularly. This land is avoided by those who can afford to live elsewhere. However, the poor are more limited in their choice – they may be forced to live in hazardous areas. By contrast, the **structuralist** school of thought stresses the constraints placed upon (poor) people by the prevailing social and political system of the country. Hence, poor people live in unsafe areas – such as on steep slopes or floodplains – because they are prevented from living in better areas.

HOW DO PEOPLE COPE WITH ENVIRONMENTAL HAZARDS?

At an individual level there are three important influences upon an individual's response:

- experience – the more experience of environmental hazards the better the adjustment to the hazard
- material well-being – those who are financially better off have more choice about how to deal with the hazard
- personality – is the person a leader or a follower, a risk-taker or risk-minimiser?

Ultimately there are three choices – do nothing and accept the hazard; adjust to the situation of living in a hazardous environment; leave the area. It is the adjustment to the hazard that is of interest.

The level of adjustment will depend, in part, upon the risks caused by the hazard. This includes:

- identification of the hazard
- estimation of the risk (probability) of the hazard
- evaluation of the cost (loss) caused by the hazard.

A number of factors influence the perception of risk (Figure 1.11).

The adjustment to the hazard includes three main options:

1 **Modify the loss burden** – spread the financial burden, e.g. insurance, disaster relief
2 **Modify the hazard event** – building design, building location, land-use zoning, emergency procedures – efforts have been made to control extreme events including flood relief schemes, seawalls, avalanche shelters, and so on
3 **Modify human vulnerability to hazard** – emergency procedures, forecasting, warning.

ENVIRONMENTAL HAZARDS AND RECURRENCE INTERVALS

Recurrence intervals are the frequency with which large or small events take place. For example, we would expect 'average' water flows in a river in the UK for much of the time – floods, however, and low flows are less common. Very large floods and severe droughts are rare, perhaps every ten to twenty years. Catastrophic floods might occur only once in every hundred years (Figure 1.12).

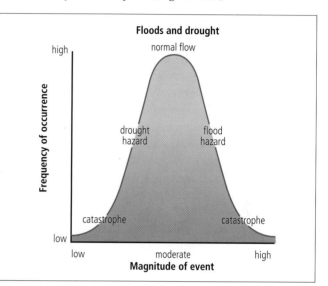

Figure 1.12 *River flows and recurrence intervals*
Source: Hewitt, K., 1997, Regions of risk: a geographical introduction to disasters, Longman

Figure 1.11 *Factors influencing public risk perception with some examples of relative safety judgments*
Source: Smith, K., 1992, Environmental hazards, Routledge

Factors tending to increase risk perception
Involuntary hazard (e.g. radioactive fallout from Chernobyl, 1986)
Immediate impact (e.g. Sydney fire, January, 1994)
Direct impact (e.g. Kobe earthquake, 1995)
Dreaded impact (e.g. cancer, AIDS)
Many fatalities per disaster (e.g. Lockerbie air crash, 1988)
Deaths grouped in space or time (e.g. Australian avalanche, 1997)
Identifiable victims (e.g. chemical plant workers, Bhopal)
Processes not well understood (e.g. nuclear accident at Sellafield, UK)
Uncontrollable hazard (e.g. Hurricane Andrew, USA, 1992)
Unfamiliar hazard (tsunami)
Lack of belief in authority (private industrialist, e.g. James Goldsmith)
Much media attention (nuclear hazards, e.g. Chernobyl, Three Mile Island, Sellafield)

Factors tending to reduce risk perception
Voluntary hazard (professional mountaineers)
Delayed impact (e.g. drought in southern Africa, 1980s/1990s)
Indirect impact (e.g. drought in Spain and the effect on tourism)
Common accident (car crash)
Few fatalities per disaster (avalanche)
Deaths random in space and time (stomach cancer)
Statistical victims (cigarette smokers)
Processes well understood (flooding)
Controllable hazard (ice on motorway)
Familiar hazard (river flood)
Belief in authority (university scientist)
Little media attention (factory discharge in water or atmosphere)

QUESTIONS

1 (a) Explain what is meant by (i) the behavioural school of thought and (ii) the structuralist school of thought.

(b) How do these two schools of thought explain why people live on flood plains?

It is possible to work out the recurrence interval for floods of certain sizes for given drainage basins by following these steps:

- collect the data of flood heights for a period of not less than thirty years
- arrange the data from high to low
- find the recurrence interval (RI) using the equation RI = (N+1) M^{-1}

where N is the number of observations

M is the rank of the individual event (highest is given rank 1).

The values can be plotted on graph paper.

Figure 1.13 shows the heights of storm surges in the Netherlands for the seventy years before the surge of February 1953. The storm of 1894 reached a height of 3.3 metres and we would expect this to occur, on average, once every seventy years. A 4 metre surge would occur, on average, once every 800 years, while the 1953 storm surge has a recurrence interval of about 500 years. This means that, on average, we would not expect another surge of the same height for about another 500 years. This is not the same as saying that there will not be one for another 500 years! Dutch planners have now built dikes which keep out all 5 metre floods, i.e. floods with a recurrence interval of once every 10 000 years.

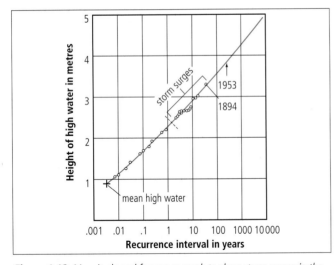

Figure 1.13 *Magnitude and frequency graph to show storm surges in the Netherlands, for seventy years before 1953*
Source: after Bryant, E., 1991, Natural hazards, Cambridge

QUESTIONS

1 Briefly state the relationship between frequency and magnitude of events.

2 Study Figure 1.13 which shows a storm magnitude and frequency graph for storm surges in the Netherlands.

a) How often would you expect a flood of about 2.8 metres in height to occur?

b) What size flood would you expect, on average, every fifty years?

THE RISING COST OF HAZARDS

One of the main inequalities in hazards is that the poor suffer most. For example, in 1996 the regions which were most affected by hazards were in developing areas such as China, where there is relatively little insurance cover. This is very true for most of the developing world, and especially for the poorer members in society.

It is not only developing countries that are at risk. Some parts of the developed world have been hard hit by the rising costs of hazards. The Kobe earthquake in Japan in 1995, for example, led to record insurance losses of US$180 billion. Similarly, in the USA, insurance companies are still reeling from the losses they suffered after the 1994 Northridge earthquake in California, and have refused to insure citizens living along the San Andreas fault.

The high cost of insurance payouts was made clear by Hurricane Andrew, which hit southern Florida in 1992. Insurers had to pay bills of over US$15 billion (£9 billion), the highest the industry had ever had to pay for a single disaster. Moreover, Hurricane Andrew was classified as a Category 4 'near miss', meaning that it was not as destructive as it could have been. The insurance bill could have been up to $60 billion, had Andrew been a stronger hurricane, Category 5, and if it had hit the commercial centre of Miami.

Since Hurricane Andrew, the USA has suffered a series of severe weather events as well as other disasters, including the 1994 Northridge earthquake, which have cost an estimated US$7 billion. Population shifts suggest higher losses could become a permanent phenomenon. In the USA, there has been a steady move of population to coastal areas, especially earthquake-prone California and hurricane-prone Florida. Other areas are at risk, too. In the New Madrid area of Missouri, earthquakes are a possibility due to faults in the area. Although the chance of an earthquake is less likely than in California, the impact could be even greater. Similarly, there is a remote possibility of a hurricane affecting Long Island, New York. Although the chances are low the impact could be catastrophic.

Although researchers are becoming better at predicting hazards and at collecting data about them, there is less understanding of why increasing numbers of people, after balancing the risks against the benefits, are deciding to live in flood zones and coastal areas where hurricanes and earthquakes are a hazard. Is a warmer and drier climate that tempting?

QUESTIONS

1 Give **two** contrasting reasons to suggest why the impact of a hurricane on Long Island (or the UK) might be catastrophic.

2 Why do few people in developing countries have adequate insurance cover against disasters? Give at least **two** contrasting reasons.

SUMMARY

We have seen that hazards result from the interaction of human and physical systems. People live in hazardous environments for a variety of reasons. There is a trade-off between economic return and social risk. For example, living in a flood plain brings advantages in the form of a ready supply of water, fertile silt, and a good communications route, but these have to be balanced against the risk of flooding.

The impact of disasters is unequal – it hits the poor more than the rich. In ELDCs there are more deaths per hazard, but less financial cost. By contrast, in EMDCs the economic cost of hazards is greater but the loss of life is much less.

Material damage, loss of life and social dislocation could be reduced substantially in most cases with reasonable planning. The choice of action is a combination of individual, community and government decision making. However, for the poor, there is often little control over what they can do to reduce the risks they face.

QUESTIONS

1 Using examples, explain why environmental hazards occur. What can be done to reduce their impact?
2 Compare and contrast the way in which environmental hazards affect EMDCs and ELDCs. Use examples and Figure 1.6 (page 7) to support your answer.

Extended (Project) work

1 For a period of two weeks, monitor any details of environmental hazards that are reported in the media. *The Guardian, Daily Mail* and *The Independent* are good sources of information. Look in detail at:

what hazards are covered
where they occur
the magnitude of the event
the number of people affected
the response to the event.

2
a) For your local area make an hazard assessment. In many settlements flooding is a problem, and increasingly, air pollution. Use Figure 1.2 (page 5) to make a classification of the hazards.
b) Devise a questionnaire to assess the perception of environmental hazards in your area. Your sample should include a mix of ages, locations and length of residence. How does the perception of hazard vary?
3 Visit your local library and research the impact of hazards in your area. Other useful sources of information are the Environment Agency, the Environmental Health Department, Engineering Department of your local City or County Council and the local Meteorological Office.

BIBLIOGRAPHY AND RECOMMENDED READING

Abbott, P., 1996, *Natural disasters*, W. C. Brown
Bryant, E., 1991, *Natural hazards*, Cambridge
Burton, I., Kates, R., and White, G., 1993, *The environment as hazard*, Guildford Press
Hewitt, K., 1997, *Regions of risk: a geographical introduction to disasters*, Longman
Park, C., 1992, *Environmental hazards*, Nelson
Smith, K., 1992, *Environmental hazards*, Routledge
Whittow, J., 1980, *Disasters*, Pelican
Wijkman, A. and Timberlake, L., 1984, *Natural disasters: Acts of God or acts of Man*, Earthscan

WEB SITES

Views of the Globe –
http://www.ngdc.noaa.gov/mgg/image/images.html
NSF Metacenter Science Highlights –
http://www.sdsc.edu/MetaScience/welcome.html
Internet Resources in the Earth Sciences –
http://www.lib.berkeley.edu/EART/EarthLinks.html

Chapter 2
Earthquakes

In this chapter we focus upon a particular hazard, that of earthquakes. We begin with an overview of the theory of plate tectonics, as this sets the scene for much of this chapter and the next chapter, Volcanoes. We look at contrasting earthquake disasters, such as Los Angeles, Maharashtra (India), Iran, Italy and Kobe (Japan). We look in detail at the Kobe disaster and analyse the primary and secondary hazards associated with the earthquake. Finally, we assess the measures that are being taken to manage the earthquake hazard. Other earthquake related hazards are treated elsewhere – for example tsunamis in Chapter 6, Coastal hazards.

THE THEORY OF PLATE TECTONICS

Plate tectonics is a group of theories developed in the 1960s and 1970s which links sea-floor spreading, continental drift, earthquake activity, volcanic activity and mountain building (Figure 2.1). It is a system which helps to explain the past and present distribution of volcanoes, earthquakes and fold mountains.

There is a growing body of scientific evidence to support the idea of continental drift (Figure 2.2).

Figure 2.1 Earthquake activity – the Iranian earthquake, 1990

Scientific evidence

- the physical 'fit' of the continents
- glacial deposits in Brazil match those in West Africa
- the geological sequence in India matches that of Antarctica
- fossil remains of an early reptile, mesosaurus, are found only in Brazil and the south west of Africa
- the reversal of magnetic particles in rocks either side of the mid-ocean ridges

Figure 2.2 The evidence for plate tectonics
Source: Nagle, G., 1998, Geography through diagrams, OUP

Figure 2.3 The world's main tectonic plates
Source: Nagle, G., 1998, Geography through diagrams, OUP

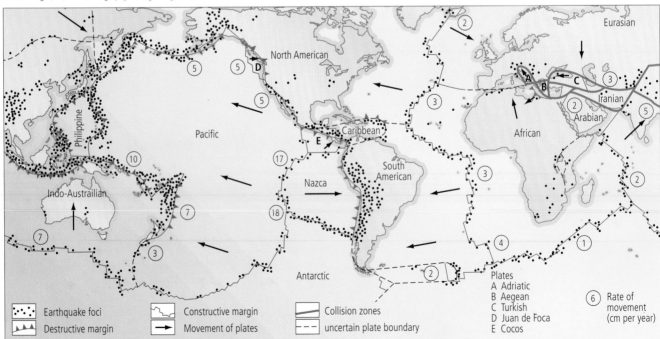

For example, drilling off the Florida coast has shown that the Bahama platform has sunk by six kilometres in the last 150 million years and that it has drifted 6000 kilometres from its former position in the South Atlantic.

The theory of plate tectonics states that the earth's crust is not continuous skin but a series of rigid caps or plates, up to 100 kilometres thick. There are seven major plates (Figure 2.3) and a series of minor plates. The plates move relative to one another, riding on a semi-molten interior or mantle.

Plates lock into each other, rather like a jigsaw. However, where they meet there is great instability because they are pushing in different directions. There are four main types of plate boundary or margin (Figure 2.4)

Type of boundary	Constructive
Processes	Two oceanic plates move apart from each other; new oceanic crust is formed in the gap, creating mid-ocean ridges; volcanic activity is common
Example	Mid-Atlantic Ridge (Europe is moving away from North America)
Type of boundary	Destructive
Processes	The oceanic plate moves towards the continental plate and sinks beneath it due to its greater density; deep sea trenches and island arcs are formed; volcanic activity is common
Example	Nazca plate sinking under the South American plate
Type of boundary	Collision
Processes	Two continental plates collide: as neither can sink they are forced up into fold mountains
Example	The Indian plate collided with the Eurasian plate to form the Himalayas
Type of boundary	Conservative
Processes	Two continental plates move sideways past each other but land is neither destroyed nor created
Example	San Andreas fault in California

Figure 2.4 *Types of plate boundary or margin*
Source: Nagle, G., 1998, Geography through diagrams, OUP

At **constructive boundaries**, (**divergent margins** or **spreading ridges**), plates move apart and fresh magma rises up from the mantle, cools, and solidifies in the gap. At this type of plate boundary, new ocean floor material is created, forming mid-ocean ridges, such as the Mid-Atlantic Ridge and the East Pacific Rise. Over time, further volumes of magma rise and force their way into the mid-ocean ridge, causing earthquakes and volcanoes. This process gradually pushes rocks on either side of the ridge apart and causes the

sea floor to spread (Figure 2.5). Consequently, the continents on either side of the ocean gradually move apart. Volcanic activity near a mid-ocean ridge can create islands such as the Azores, Ascension Island and Tristan da Cunha. As the sea floor spreads, these islands can be carried away from the centre of the ocean.

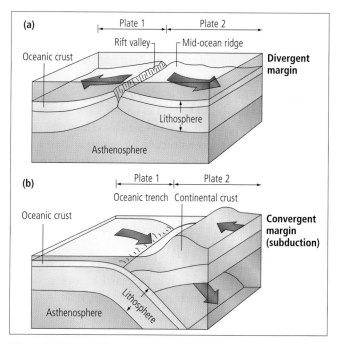

Figure 2.5(a) and (b) *Constructive and destructive plate boundaries*
Source: Skinner, B. and Porter, S., 1995, The dynamic earth, Wiley

At **destructive boundaries** (**convergent** or **subduction margins**), two plates meet and the heavier or less buoyant plate plunges under the lighter or more buoyant plate. Where oceanic crust and continental crust converge, the denser oceanic crust (denser because it is cooler and composed of silica and magnesium) plunges under the lighter, less dense continental crust (composed largely of silica and aluminium). Where the plates meet a **subduction zone** is created. At a subduction zone there is a deep seafloor trench, such as the Marianas Trench, in the north west Pacific and the Aleutian Trench, in the north east Pacific. As the oceanic plate descends, it carries the crust back into the mantle. Much of the crust material melts at depths of between 100 kilometres and 300 kilometres and is changed to magma by 700 kilometres. As the plate melts, magma rises under very high pressure and escapes through fissures in the crumpled sediments of the continental crust running parallel to the ocean trench.

A good example is along the west coast of South America where the oceanic Nazca plate dives under the continental South American plate. The Andes chain of fold mountains, formed by the crumpling of sediments as the plates pushed together, experiences strong earthquake and volcanic activity. Where the subduction takes place under the ocean (as opposed to under a continent), island arcs, associated with extensive earthquake and volcanic activity (Figure 2.5b on page 13), are formed, as in the case of Japan and the Philippines.

Collision boundaries occur when plates are too buoyant or thick to subduct, for example, where two continental plates converge. In this case, the sediments that are trapped between the plates become folded and faulted. This is thought to be how the Alps and the Himalayas were formed.

Conservative boundaries (**passive** or **transform margins**) occur when two plates glide past each other with no formation or destruction of crust. The most notable example is the San Andreas fault in California. These boundaries are associated with intense earthquake activity.

Many plates have a constructive boundary on one side, a destructive one on the other and transform boundaries on the remaining sides.

Plate movement

There are a number of reasons why plates move. These include:

- **convection currents**
  these currents deep within the earth's core produce plumes of magma, which rise through the mantle. These force their way up to the surface, pushing apart overlying rock. Radioactive decay is thought to be responsible for the convection currents.
- **dragging**
  Plates are dragged down (subducted) by their oldest edge or leading edge which has become cold and heavy. Plates are hot at the mid-ocean ridge but as they move away they become cooler and heavier.

EARTHQUAKES

An earthquake is a series of shocks and tremors that result from a sudden release of pressure. Every year there are some 3000 earthquakes of at least moderate intensity, but most cause little damage. Whether or not they cause serious damage and major loss of life has as much to do with where the earthquake happens as with its size. Earthquakes are most frequently found in areas where two plates are moving against each other, or where there is volcanic activity (Figure 2.6). In addition, human activity can lead to earthquakes. Underground explosions, nuclear testing, mining, drilling and the construction of large dams have all been linked with an increase in earthquake activity. This is because these kinds of human activity create shock waves and significant pressure changes in the underlying rock strata.

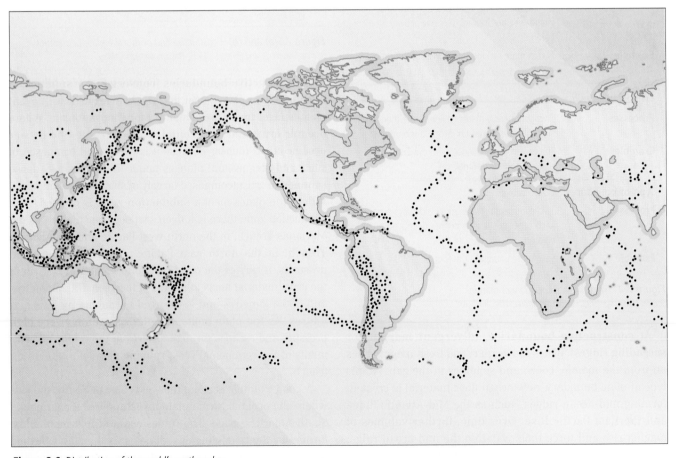

Figure 2.6 *Distribution of the world's earthquakes*
Source: Ollier, C., 1988, Volcanoes, Blackwell

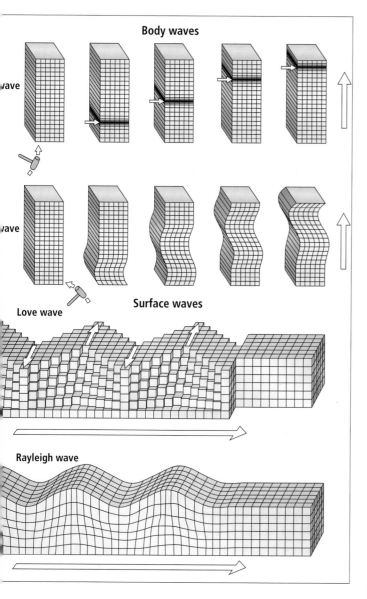

Love wave

Surface waves

Rayleigh wave

Figure 2.7 *Types of shock wave*
Source: Robinson, A., 1993, Earthshock, Thames and Hudson

The magnitude and intensity of earthquakes are measured by the Richter Scale and the Mercalli Modified Mercalli Intensity Scale. Earthquake magnitude is usually measured on the Richter scale. This is a logarithmic scale, meaning that each unit represents a 10-fold increase in the size of the earthquake's power and energy. Thus an earthquake of magnitude 2 is ten times as powerful as one of magnitude l. Earthquakes in the UK (for example, in Devon in October 1997) only reach 2.5-4.5 on the Richter Scale. The Assissi earthquake in 1997 was 5.5, and the strongest ever recorded was 8.4, in China. The intensity of earthquakes is measured on the Mercalli scale. This is a qualitative index of the effects of the earthquake on ground vibration and structural damage.

The magnitude and intensity of an earthquake depend upon a number of factors:

- the depth at which the shock originates – earthquakes which occur near the earth's surface have a greater effect, because the movements are greater, and there is less time to warn people
- the nature of the overlying materials – where the rock is loosely consolidated, the shock is most intensive
- the nature of the terrain – steep mountain slopes or flat coastal plains intensify the effects of an earthquake. On steep mountain slopes, it may cause many landslides, particularly if there is unconsolidated material on the surface. On coastal plains, soils may offer poor building foundations; alluvial materials can amplify shock waves and may turn into liquid (**liquefaction**) if the vibrations are intense enough, buildings fall apart and can even sink into the soil
- the number of people and types of building in the earthquake area.

EARTHQUAKES IN ELDCs

In ELDCs the impact of earthquakes is often greater than in EMDCs. This is because in ELDCs, building standards may be poor, and emergency services not as developed as in ELDCs. Also, many places are remote and isolated. This means that some rescue services may not reach the location of the disaster for many hours – in the case of the Iranian earthquake, up to 72-96 hours, and in the case of Rostaq, Afghanistan (in 1998), over a week.

Earthquakes are related to waves within the earth's interior. Two main types of waves occur, body waves and surface waves (Figure 2.7). Body waves are transmitted upwards to the surface from the centre of the earthquake. Primary (P) waves are the fastest, and can move through solids and liquids. Secondary (S) waves move with a sideways motion, and are unable to move through liquids. They make the ground move horizontally, hence they cause much damage. When P-waves and S-waves reach the surface, some of them are transformed into surface waves. These can cause the ground to move sideways (Love Waves) or up and down (Rayleigh Waves).

QUESTIONS

1 Explain briefly what takes place **(i)** at a mid-ocean ridge and **(ii)** in a subduction zone.

2 Describe the distribution of earthquakes as shown on Figure 2.6.

3 What kind of plate boundary is the San Andreas fault? What tectonic process is taking place there?

Iranian earthquake, June 1990

On 21 June 1990, northern Iran was devastated by an earthquake of magnitude 7.3. The final death toll was over 50 000. Rescue work was hampered by a series of **aftershocks** (smaller, secondary earthquakes) and by **secondary** hazards, such as landslides in the mountains and disease epidemics. The steep terrain contributed to the large number of deaths by increasing the intensity of the earthquake and causing landslides.

The Caspian region of Iran is a text-book case of an earthquake calamity that was waiting to happen. There are a number of plates in the area, and scientists believe there are many unknown plate boundaries in the region (local faults). Pressure had been building up for decades, and finally the pressure was released in the 1990 earthquake. The combination of rapidly rising population and 'local warfare' meant that building standards designed to cope with earthquakes had not been followed – there was less reinforcement of building structures and much mud and brick housing. Before the Islamic revolution in 1979, Iran's population numbered 35 million. This increased rapidly to 55 million with Tehran doubling in size to over 8 million. Building standards designed to cope with earthquakes had not been followed in the strife-torn years.

Some of the worst hit areas were on the low-lying Caspian plains, where the death toll was highest. The potential for disaster was magnified by the attraction of the fertile soil for farmers – more than four million people grow most of Iran's food there; and its use for building developments – towns and cities had expanded in river valleys and coastal regions on the relatively flat land.

Iranian earthquake, May 1997

In May 1997, over 2400 people were killed and over 6000 were injured in an earthquake which affected a mountainous area in the north-east of Iran (Figure 2.8). Thousands were made homeless by the earthquake which measured 7.1 on the Richter scale. It was followed by more than 130 aftershocks. Most of the damage was in a 90 kilometre stretch between Birjand and Qaen, a region characterised by poor villages and mud huts. In the village of Ardakul, about 90 kilometres east of Qaen, more than 500 of the 1600 inhabitants were killed during the earthquake and the aftershocks.

Iranian officials appealed for aid to help the 40 000 people made homeless. Much of the aid donated from the west took three or four days to reach the area – the critical period of need is the first twenty-four hours, often when there is limited water and power availability. Much of the 'aid' was provided by the villagers themselves – by providing shelter in their own homes for homeless families and helping with the rebuilding programme. By contrast, in EMDCs, such as

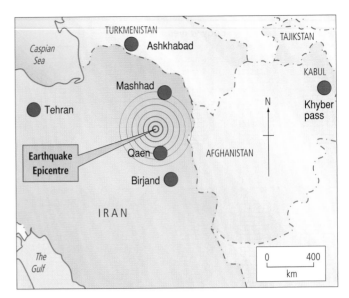

Figure 2.8 *The Iranian earthquake, 1997*
Source: The Guardian, May 1997

the USA, more of the reconstruction programme is carried out directly by the state.

The earthquake was Iran's worst since 1990; considerable damage is also believed to have occurred in neighbouring Afghanistan, although there are few details available.

The Indian earthquake of 1993

India's worst earthquake for fifty years, in terms of its death toll, and the nation's worst natural disaster of any kind for twenty years, occurred on 30 September 1993. More than 25 000 people died, and many thousands more were unaccounted for, after fifty towns and villages over an area of 13 000 square kilometres in the state of Maharashtra, were devastated (Figure 2.9). The shock measured 6.4 on the Richter scale.

Like the Iranian earthquake in 1990, the epicentre was shallow so that the shock waves reached the surface quickly. The earthquake happened in the night when almost all the victims were indoors and asleep. It occurred in a region almost totally unprepared for earthquakes, and building standards regulations were unlikely to have been enforced. Moreover, as we saw in Book 1 of this series, *Development and Underdevelopment*, Maharashtra is a growth region in India and has experienced huge population growth.

The last earthquake in the region was in 1967 at Koyna, near Bombay. This one had almost certainly been initiated by the filling of a new reservoir with billions of tons of water. Reservoirs ponded back to a height of more than 100 metres are now thought to trigger earthquakes. Where there are large dams, the increased weight of water causes a build up of pressure on the undelrying rocks. It is this increased pressure which can cause earthquakes.

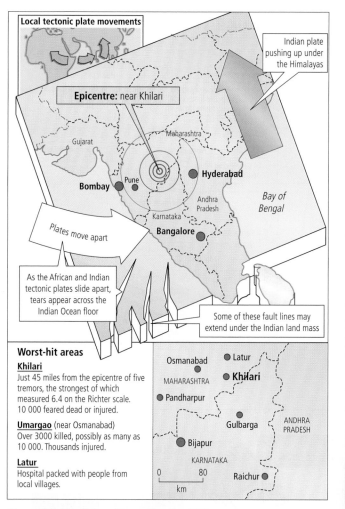

Local tectonic plate movements

Indian plate pushing up under the Himalayas

Epicentre: near Khilari

Gujarat

Maharashtra

Hyderabad

Bombay
Pune

Andhra
Pradesh

Bay of
Bengal

Karnataka

Bangalore

Plates move apart

As the African and Indian tectonic plates slide apart, tears appear across the Indian Ocean floor

Some of these fault lines may extend under the Indian land mass

Worst-hit areas

Khilari
Just 45 miles from the epicentre of five tremors, the strongest of which measured 6.4 on the Richter scale. 10 000 feared dead or injured.

Umargao (near Osmanabad)
Over 3000 killed, possibly as many as 10 000. Thousands injured.

Latur
Hospital packed with people from local villages.

Osmanabad
Latur

MAHARASHTRA   Khilari

Pandharpur

Gulbarga   ANDHRA
PRADESH

Bijapur

KARNATAKA

0   80

km

Raichur

Figure 2.9 The Maharashtra earthquake, 1993
Source: The Guardian, October 1993

Part of the problem in the 1997 earthquake was caused by building developments in the state. Traditional village houses are made of mud reinforced with wattle or bamboo. These structures have lightweight roofs and their occupants are less at risk from collapsing buildings. Ironically, however, the villagers of eastern Maharashtra were wealthy enough to build their homes in stone and brick with cement roofs. Several cities of over 500 000 people had also sprung up in the region. Most of their homes had been assembled from breeze blocks and concrete, many constructed without permission and unsupervised.

QUESTIONS

1 Why is Iran subject to earthquake activity?

2 Study Figure 2.9 which shows some of the causes and the consequences of the Maharashtra earthquake in 1993.

a) What was the cause of the earthquake?

b) Briefly describe **two** ways in which Maharashtra's status as a growth region influenced the disaster.

3 What are the similarities in the causes and the effects of the Iranian earthquake in 1997 and the Indian earthquake of 1993?

EARTHQUAKES IN EMDCs

Los Angeles earthquake, USA, 1994

In January 1994, a major earthquake struck Los Angeles, California. The earthquake was caused by the movement of a minor fault. Centred near Northridge in the San Fernando Valley (Figure 2.11 on page 18), it caused US$15 billion damage in nearby Los Angeles, and almost sixty deaths. (This compares with tens of thousands who died in Iran and Maharashtra.) The main shock was recorded as 6.6 on the Richter scale. Damage was of disastrous proportions: flattened buildings, shattered bridges and roads; ruptured gas, electricity and water mains with consequential fires and floods. The death toll would certainly have been higher had the earthquake not occurred in the early hours of a public holiday, at a time when people were away on holiday, and there were fewer people on the highways. The disaster forced earthquake engineers to re-examine the design of office buildings, bridges and overpasses, because the damage, particularly to roads, was worse than had been expected.

In California the communities are wealthy compared to those in Iran and India, they are better prepared for earthquakes, and building standards are high (Figure 2.12 on page 18). Disastrous losses of life in recent years have all been in poor countries with inadequate building standards.

Figure 2.10 The Los Angeles earthquake of January 1994

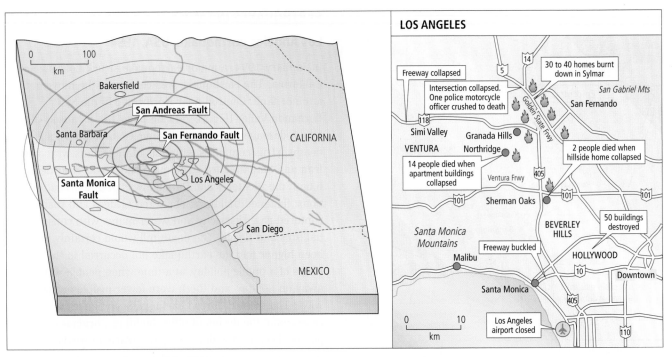

Figure 2.11 *The Los Angeles earthquake, 1994*
Source: The Independent, January 1994

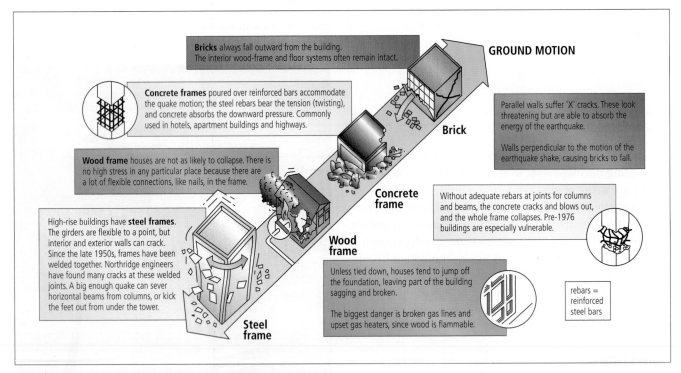

Figure 2.12 *Damage to buildings of different construction in an earthquake*
Source: Nagle, G. and Spencer, K., 1996, Investigating geography, Hodder and Stoughton

QUESTIONS

1 Why is southern California subject to earthquake activity?

2 Explain why the damage done by the earthquake was so costly, but relatively few lives were lost.

3 How does this compare with the earthquakes in Iran and India? Give reasons for your answer.

Case study:
The Kobe earthquake, Japan, January 1995

Each year Japan experiences more earthquakes than any other country owing to its position on the Pacific Ring of Fire (Figure 2.13). Along the east of Japan the Pacific Ocean plate is descending below the Eurasian plate at a rate of about ten centimetres per year. This has formed a subduction trench of up to eight kilometres deep running parallel to Japan's eastern coastline. At the same time, off the south-east coast of Japan, the Pacific plate is being subducted beneath the Philippine plate, which is itself being subducted beneath southern Japan.

The earthquake in Kobe in the Hanshin region of Japan on 17th January 1995, killed over 5000 people, injured over 30 000 people and made almost a third of a million people homeless. Nearly 60% of those who died were sixty years and older. They died mostly as a result of suffocation or being crushed. It occurred at 5.46 a.m. which helped to limit the number of deaths. The earthquake was shallow – fourteen kilometres below the earth's surface. It registered 7.2 on the Richter scale and caused a great deal of destruction due to vertical and horizontal shaking.

Many important public facilities, such as the City Hall and public hospitals were damaged, or collapsed. In addition, 80% of the schools, museums, sports facilities and sake breweries were severely damaged. Housing damage was extensive. Of a total of 472 160 houses before the earthquake:
- 67 421 were fully destroyed
- 55 145 were partially destroyed
- 6965 were completely burnt
- 80 were half burnt
- 270 were partially burnt.

Over 235 000 people were evacuated during January 1995. These people were housed in 600 shelters – mostly prefabricated, and provided after the earthquake. By August 1995, just under 7000 people were being housed in shelters.

The earthquake came as a surprise to Japanese seismologists, because the Hanshin region was thought to be one of the safest areas in Japan in terms of seismic activity. It was the most serious earthquake since the 1923 Tokyo earthquake when over 140 000 people were killed. Japanese engineers are keenly aware of the problems of earthquake activity and have designed modern buildings so that they are either mounted on shock absorbing rubber or else can sway with the motion of earthquake activity. However, buildings which date from the early 1960s or before do not have these innovations and they have suffered the most damage and destruction.

Conditions worsened for Kobe's survivors as rain, strong winds and lightning increased the risk of landslides, and doctors were faced with outbreaks of disease due to the damp, unhygienic conditions people were forced to live in.

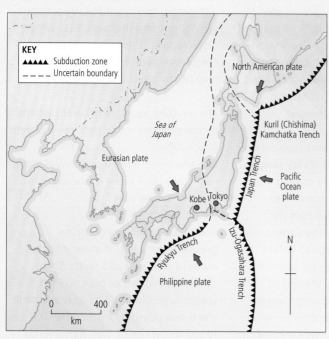

Figure 2.13 *The location of Kobe, Hanshin, in relation to plate boundaries*
Source: Geofile, April, 1996

Figure 2.14 *Secondary hazards at Kobe – fire*

Indeed, the immediate effects of the earthquake, i.e. destruction of buildings and loss of life were only part of the problem. **Secondary** effects such as fires, ruptured gas- and water-supplies intensified the hazard, and aftershocks toppled structures weakened in the initial earthquake (Figure 2.14 on page 19). Over 1320 aftershocks were recorded, of which 150 could be felt. There were 175 fires as a result of the earthquake, 59 of these occurring simultaneously during the earthquake. Over 80 hectares were burnt. Many people lost families, friends, possessions and livelihoods. The chances of rebuilding homes in the Kobe area are limited because most people in the region were not covered by home insurance.

In addition to all the quantifiable aspects of the earthquake, there were many unquantifiable effects. People suffered as a result of evacuation, long periods of residence in evacuation shelters, disruptions in schooling, increased levels of unemployment, worry, stress and mental fatigue.

Figure 2.15 Homeless people in a shelter at Kobe

Services were badly affected:

- power cuts affected the whole city until 23 January
- up to 25% of phone lines damaged
- water supplies were disrupted until April
- up to 80% of gas supplies were affected – these were not fully restored for nearly three months
- three of the city's seven sewage treatment plants were damaged or stopped working (they were restored in May the same year)
- waste disposal services were disrupted for over a month.

Traffic was severely disrupted (Figure 2.15). Sinking ground, cracks and collapsed buildings made travelling hazardous. Railways were damaged in many places and access routes to Kobe were interrupted. Over 130 kilometres of bullet train network was closed, and the Hanshin Expressway was completely closed when a 1-kilometre stretch of the elevated highway collapsed. The city's port was severely disrupted and throughout the region employment opportunities were reduced. The economic cost of the earthquake was estimated at about £80 billion. Many of Kobe's manufacturers were crippled by the earthquake. About 80% of the shoe factories, which are quite important in the region, were damaged, over 50% of the breweries were seriously damaged, and one-third of Kobe's shopping district was seriously damaged.

A few years after the earthquake there are still evacuation shelters for people who have not been able to return to homes. The City Government has introduced a 'Three Year Plan for Restoring Houses after the Earthquake'. This replaces plans they had before the earthquake and will see an additional 72 000 houses built. By the end of 1996, over 60 000 houses had been cleared away. Altogether, more than 10 million cubic metres of rubble were created by the earthquake.

By mid-1997 most of the manufacturing capacity had been restored; up to 90% of shoe manufacturers have reopened, and sales at retail outlets had risen to 80% of pre-earthquake levels. However, many firms that survived the earthquake decided to relocate from Kobe to safer premises.

Earthquake countermeasures in Japan

Since the Kobe earthquake, Japan has responded to the threat of earthquakes in a number of ways. Measures include:

- making buildings and cities more able to cope with disasters (Figure 2.16),
- reinforcement of the disaster prevention systems and increasing the awareness of the disaster prevention
- promotion of earthquake prediction.

A single-storey building (A) has a quick response to earthquake forces, whereas a high-rise building responds slowly, and shock waves are amplified as they move up the structure. If the buildings are too close, vibrations may be amplified between buildings. A stepped profile offers greater stability. Asymmetrical buildings (D and E) are often twisted during an earthquake, and experience differential rocking. If the various parts are not put together well, they will be pulled apart. Often a design, such as a car park or pedestrian access, (as in F) may be the weak link in the design.

The weakest parts are generally where connections are made between different structural elements. This, in part, explains why elevated motorways are at risk – they have many connecting welds and reinforcing bars.

The sites which cause particular problems are areas of unconsolidated material, soft soils and faults. These should be avoided or built on with special care. Cut and fill techniques limit the threat posed by earthquakes (by reducing the risk of mass movements) while an earthquake frame (J and K) or

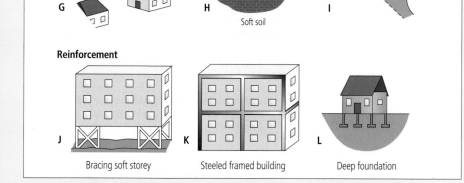

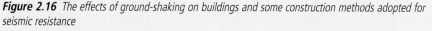

Figure 2.16 *The effects of ground-shaking on buildings and some construction methods adopted for seismic resistance*
Source: Smith, K., 1992, Environmental hazards, Routledge

- Emergency Plan for Earthquake Disaster Prevention.

This also laid down the areas designated as in need of monitoring. The Act also provided the financial assistance needed for such programmes.

A repeat of Tokyo's 1923 earthquake would be catastrophic. Then, the Great Kanto earthquake started a fire that burned for three days in Tokyo, killing about 140 000 people and destroying 370 000 buildings. Now Tokyo is one of the world's largest and most densely populated cities. There are huge stores of chemicals, petroleum, oil and liquefied gas. A large proportion of the housing is made of wood and 65% of the city is below sea level on reclaimed land.

The absence of a large earthquake in the South Kanto area increases the possibility of a destructive earthquake hitting it in the near future. Many of the socio-economic activities and functions of Japan are concentrated in this area. It accounts for over 33% of Japan's gross national product and 25% of its population. In addition, Tokyo is a World City (a city of international standing) and has an increasingly important role in world finance and the world economy.

Earthquake prediction has been carried out systematically in Japan since 1964. Since 1969 two areas have been designated as centres of intensive observation and a further eight areas receive special observation (Figure 2.17, on page 22).

The Areas of Special Observation are areas which:
- have had a large-scale earthquake in living memory, but not recently
- are in an active tectonic area
- have recently experienced active crustal movement
- have critical social importance, such as Tokyo.

deep foundation (L) will help to stabilise an area.

Four measures have been used to help cities cope in the event of an earthquake:
1 securing and improving evacuation sites and routes
2 promoting fire-resistant construction of buildings and improving fire-fighting facilities
3 upgrading aseismatic standards for buildings, enforcing standards at public facilities
4 improving prediction and monitoring of earthquakes in disaster prevention centres.

The 'Large-scale Earthquake Counter-measures Act' of 1978 created the:
- Basic Plan for Earthquakes
- Earthquake Disaster Prevention

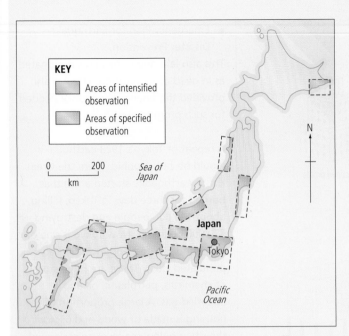

Figure 2.17 *Areas of intensified and special earthquake observation in Japan*

The Areas of Intensified Observation are areas which require further research to clarify the cause when abnormalities are observed.

In the Tokai area and its vicinity, the southern central area near Tokyo, there is a continuous earthquake observation network. In this area, large-scale earthquakes have occurred repeatedly, as a result of the subduction of the Philippine and Pacific plates beneath the Eurasian plate. In the area of the Suruga Bay more than 130 years have elapsed since the last earthquake, so the possibility of a large-scale earthquake occurring in the near future is thought to be high.

QUESTIONS

1   From information in this section what do you think the term 'aseismatic' means?

2   Why are fires such a hazard after an earthquake? Explain at least two contrasting reasons why this is a problem in Tokyo.

3   There is a large amount of reclaimed land in Tokyo. Why is this land at risk from earthquakes?

4   Why is Japan prone to earthquake activity?

5   Kobe's earthquake occurred before the rush hour. Had it occurred during the rush hour a much greater loss of life would have resulted. Why is this so?

6   What is an 'aftershock'? How does it compare in magnitude to the initial earthquake?

7   Explain why so few buildings were covered by insurance in Kobe.

8   Choose an appropriate method to show the housing damage that occurred in the Kobe earthquake.

The Italian earthquake, 1997

During September 1997, more than 400 earth tremors were recorded in the central Italian region around Assisi (Figure 2.18). Two powerful earthquakes, measuring 5.6 and 4.8 on the Richter scale, struck central Italy on September 26, 1997 killing eleven people, injuring over 125 people and forcing 100 000 people to leave their homes. Up to 70% of the buildings in Assisi were evacuated due to safety fears. However, the earthquake was newsworthy for other reasons – it badly damaged priceless thirteenth and fourteenth century paintings in the Basilica of St Francis of Assisi (Figure 2.19).

Since 1900 there have been nineteen severe earthquakes in Italy, killing over 120 000 people. Italy is close to a number of plates – the Adriatic, Eurasian and African plates. This earthquake, although only minor in its impact on the loss of human life, has been one of the very few to affect Italian

heritage. Although media attention focused upon the Basilica of St Francis, all across the region medieval churches and towers have been reduced to rubble. Since 1945, earthquakes have cost Italy over US$100 billion. For example, the 1976 earthquake, which shook the north-east of the country, killed over 1000 people, and in the Naples area in 1980 an earthquake killed nearly 3000 people.

Some local villagers complained that rescue operations were slow and inadequate and that priority was given to Assisi because of its paintings. The history of earthquakes in Italy had spared Italian works of art until this latest earthquake. Perhaps, as a consequence, little precaution had been taken in areas of outstanding artistic and cultural heritage. That is no longer the case.

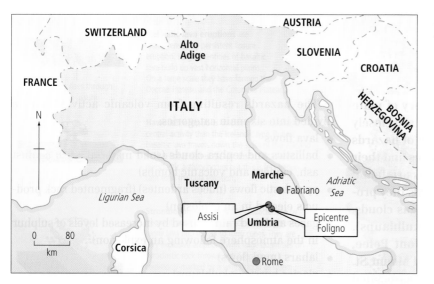

Figure 2.18 *Location of the Italian earthquake, 1997*
Source: The Times, September 27, 1997

Figure 2.19 *Damage at the Basilica of St. Francis, Assisi*

SUMMARY

In this chapter we have outlined the nature of plate tectonics. In particular, we focused upon earthquakes and their associated hazards. We have seen that earthquakes can occur anywhere in the world wherever there is a build up and release of pressure. This mostly takes place at plate boundaries. We have also seen how the effect of earthquakes varies with the strength and intensity of the shock, its depth beneath the earth's surface, the nature of the bedrock (hard or unconsolidated), the nature of the terrain (steep or flat), and the type of country involved (developed versus less developed). Much also depends upon chance factors, such as the time of day when the earthquake occurs. However, there are many precautions that can be taken to reduce the impact of earthquakes, although some of these can only be afforded by developed countries. Hazards, it would seem, affect the poor disproportionately.

QUESTIONS

1 In what ways is it possible to forecast earthquake activity? How useful and accurate are these methods?

2 Describe and explain a number of contrasting reasons why it may be difficult to evacuate an area known to be experiencing earthquakes.

3 With the use of examples, illustrate the economic, social, environmental and political costs associated with earthquake activity. For example, compare and contrast the effects of the 1997 Iranian and Italian earthquakes.

BIBLIOGRAPHY AND RECOMMENDED READING

Abbott, P., 1996, *Natural disasters*, William Brown Publishing

Bryant, E., 1991, *Natural hazards*, Cambridge

Fielding Smith, A & Smith, R., 1996, *Earthquakes – an update* Geofile, 282

National Land Agency, 1991, *Disaster countermeasures in Japan*, Government of Japan

WEB SITES

World earthquakes –
    http://gldfs.cr.usgs.gov/
World quakes –
    http://www.civeng.carleton.ca/cgi-bin/quakes/
Southern California earthquake center –
    http://www.scecdc.scec.org/
Northern California earthquake data –
    http://quake.geo.berkeley.edu

LEVELS OF VOLCANIC ACTIVITY

Active volcanoes are volcanoes which continue to erupt or be at risk of erupting. **Extinct** volcanoes have stopped erupting, and **dormant** volcanoes are those which have not erupted for a very long time but could still erupt. It is an arbitrary classification, and the distinction between dormant and extinct is difficult to define.

The amount of silica in the lava makes the difference between volcanoes which erupt continuously, such as those on Iceland and Hawaii, where silica levels are low, and those where eruptions are infrequent but violent, such as in Japan and the Philippines, where silica levels are high. Silica levels are determined by the location of the volcano – lava released where the oceans meet the continents absorbs silica-rich sediments: this causes the lava to become less viscous and block the vents until enough pressure has built up to break them open.

The following examples illustrate the range of hazards experienced during and after volcanic activity, and the responses to these hazards. We begin with an example from the USA, the eruption of Mount St. Helens in 1980.

'A SAINT SHE AIN'T': MOUNT ST. HELENS, 1980

In March 1980 Mount St. Helens (Figure 3.3) resumed volcanic activity after a dormant period of some 123 years. A series of small earthquakes began and these were monitored daily. The cause of the activity was the subduction (dragging down) of the Juan de Fuca plate beneath the North American plate. Scientists predicted that the volcano could erupt at any time and, in response, the area was closed to tourists and sightseers. On 18 May, Mount St. Helens erupted, killing 62 people, most of whom had managed to gain access to restricted areas to obtain a better view of the volcano.

Figure 3.3 *Mount St. Helens before the eruption*

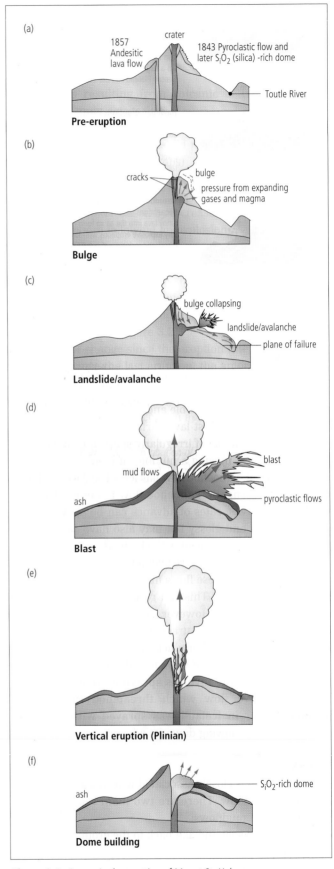

Figure 3.4 *Stages in the eruption of Mount St. Helens*
Source: Abbott, P., 1996, Natural disasters, William Brown

The explosion took place following a long sequence of events (Figure 3.4). The previous eruption, in 1857, had created weaknesses within the volcanic cone (a). Over a hundred years later, rising magma and gas changed the shape of the volcano as it began to bulge (b). On 18 May, 1980, an earthquake which registered 5.1 on the Richter scale triggered a massive landslide and avalanche (c). Over 2.5 cubic kilometres of the mountain was carried away in flows that reached 250 kilometres per hour. Lahars caused by rain and melting snow carried magma, ice, rocks, and trees into Spirit Lake, causing waves 200 metres high. When the debris was finally deposited, it reached depths of 45 metres. As the lahars moved away from Mount St. Helens, the tremendous reduction of pressure caused an enormous blast and pyroclastic flows, which, at temperatures of over 300°C, travelled at speeds of over 400 kilometres per hour (d). An area of over 500 square kilometres was scorched. This blast in turn opened up the crater of the volcano which allowed a further eruption (e) of gas and magma. The escaping gas reached heights of 20 kilometres.

Since then, the volcano has been rebuilding a new dome rich in acidic magma, (rich in silica, SiO_2) (f) and has changed out of all recognition (Figure 3.5). Given the size of the event, the number of deaths was relatively small and the amount of destruction was also limited.

Figure 3.5 *Mount St. Helens after the eruption*

QUESTIONS

1 Explain why volcanic activity occurs along the Cascades Range of mountains in USA.

2 Give **two** reasons why so few people were killed by the Mount St. Helens eruption.

3 Using an atlas explain why the amount of damage was relatively small.

MOUNT PINATUBO AND THE PACIFIC RING OF FIRE

Three-quarters of the earth's 550 historically active volcanoes lie along the Pacific Ring of Fire (Figure 3.6). This includes most of the world's recent volcanoes, including Mount Pinatubo in the Philippines (Figure 3.7). Indeed, the Philippines, an arc of islands found at the edge of an ocean plate, are beset by a variety of environmental hazards including cyclones, landslides, tsunami (waves generated by tectonic activity), earthquakes and volcanoes. However, without volcanic activity the Philippines would not exist: they consist of the remains of previous eruptions.

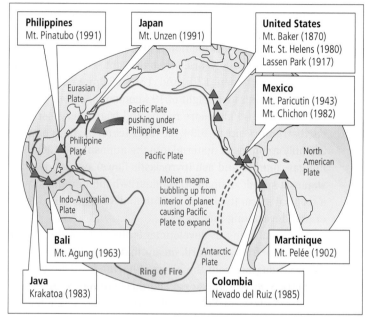

Figure 3.6 *Pacific Ring of Fire*
Source: Nagle, G.,1998, Geography through diagrams, OUP

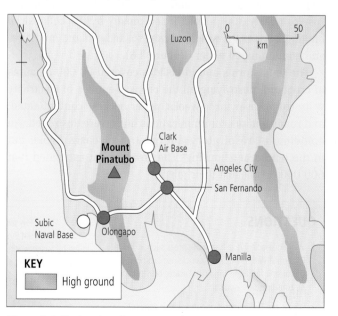

Figure 3.7 *The location of Mount Pinatubo*
Source: Nagle, G. and Spencer, K., 1996, Investigating geography, Hodder and Stoughton

In June 1991, two major volcanic eruptions occurred, attracting world-wide attention. The first, Mount Unzen near Nagasaki in Japan, had been predicted from scientific monitoring. It was known to be only dormant and was therefore monitored for signs of impending eruption. During a previous eruption in 1792, 15 000 people perished. In 1991, by contrast, an orderly evacuation of the local population took place, although 39 people died, including a geologist and several journalists there to observe and report the event for the news media. The second eruption was of Mount Pinatubo just one week later, which had been assumed to be extinct.

In April and May 1991 a number of small eruptions around Mount Pinatubo showed that this was not so. In May, swarms of small earthquakes also took place. On June 9th, the 1460 metre volcanic dome, which had remained dormant for almost 600 years, began to erupt. The most serious eruptions, between 12th and 15th of June, blew rock, pumice and ash to a height of 19 kilometres, before scattering it over a 100 kilometre radius and triggering a series of earth tremors up to 5.34 on the Richter scale, spewing 20 million tonnes of material into the atmosphere. Clouds of hot gas, pumice and ash (pyroclastic flows) swept down the slopes at speeds of up to 80 kilometres/hour. Combined with a tropical storm (typhoon) on 15th and 16th of June, it generated devastating mudslides.

The monitoring of developments throughout the Pacific Ring of Fire from the April, meant that over 200 000 people were evacuated from the area, unharmed. By June 10th, 14 500 US service personnel and their families were evacuated from Clark Air Base to Subic Naval Base, 40 kilometres south-west of Pinatubo. By June 22nd, 20 000 dependents of US personnel had been evacuated to the USA. The initial death toll was low – six confirmed deaths. However, the toll rose to nearly 350 people, killed mostly by the collapse of buildings under the weight of rain-soaked ash and mud, fire, and contaminated water (Figure 3.8).

The mud storms and mudslides covered 50 000 hectares of cropland, destroying all the crops. Supplies of electricity were cut for over three weeks, water became contaminated, and roads and telecommunications links were destroyed. An epidemic of respiratory and gastric diseases broke out in the temporary housing. The government estimated that 600 000 people lost their jobs.

Figure 3.8 *Mudslides engulfed settlements in the Philippines following the eruption of Mount Pinatubo*

It is believed the eruption was triggered by a major earthquake, measuring 7.7 on the Richter scale, that occurred on 16th July, 1990. This earthquake rocked Manilla and the surrounding region, killing 1600 people and injuring a further 3000. The earthquake allowed basalt from the upper mantle to squeeze into the magma chamber full of viscous lava. The basalt reactivated the magma and produced a fluid, gas-charged magma called andesite. This rose towards the surface causing the volcano to bulge. Pressure increased continuously until it grew to be sufficient to blast the dome away.

MONT PELÉE, MARTINIQUE, 1902

Mont Pelée is located on the northern edge of the island of Martinique in the Caribbean. The area has a complex tectonic setting (Figure 3.9). The name 'Pelée' means 'bald' or 'peeled', a reference to the lack of vegetation on the top of Mont Pelée – destroyed by eruptions in 1792 and 1851.

The pyroclastic flows from Mont Pelée that destroyed the town of St. Pierre in 1902 illustrate not only the immense power of volcanoes but also the human element in turning a hazard into a disaster.

QUESTIONS

1 Why do people live in hazardous areas such as Mount Pinatubo? With the use of examples explain how **(i)** volcanic landforms and **(ii)** volcanic activity can be considered a resource.

2 Why is the Philippines prone to volcanic activity?

3 Explain why so few people were killed by the initial blast of the Mount Pinatubo eruption but were killed in the following weeks. Up to a million livestock died as a result of the eruption. How, and why, do you think they died?

4 Study Figure 3.6 which shows the Pacific Ring of Fire. Describe the location of the volcanoes shown on the map. How do they vary with **(i)** constructive and **(ii)** destructive plate margins? Identify any areas where volcanic activity is not associated with plate margins. How do you account for this?

5 What evidence is there to suggest that earthquakes may trigger volcanoes and vice versa?

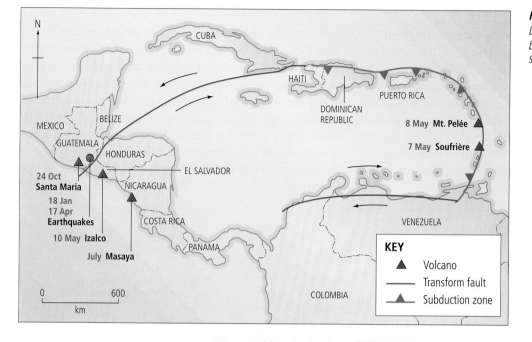

Figure 3.9
Location of Mont Pelée and plate boundaries in the Caribbean
Source: Bryant, E., 1991, Natural hazards

Figure 3.10 *The devastation of St. Pierre was caused by the eruption of Mont Pelée, 1902*

Volcanic activity took place in 1792, then again in 1851 and resumed in 1902. The magma rising within the volcano was very viscous and plugged the vent to the crater. This meant that eruptions were sporadic rather than continuous and occurred only when pressure built up sufficiently to force the top off the vent. This gave rise to a series of periodic volcanic blasts. During April and early May, 1902, it became obvious that volcanic activity was increasing. Large numbers of people left the rural areas and headed for the perceived safety of St. Pierre.

On May 5th a pyroclastic flow travelled down the valley of the Riviere Blanche, destroying a sugar mill and killing 40 people; over 150 people were drowned in surrounding fields. The pyroclastic flow contained a 35 metre wave of mud. When the wave hit the ocean, it created a tsunami which killed over 100 people in St. Pierre. At this time the town should have been evacuated. However, an election was due on 10th May and the governor, Governor Mouttet, feared that he would not be re-elected if a large proportion of the electorate were absent on polling day. He moved into the town to reassure people that it was safe.

Mont Pelée erupted again on 6th May. Ash and tephra destroyed homes and buildings and clogged roads. Mass panic descended on the town and the governor used troops to prevent mass evacuation.

On the morning of 8th May, Mont Pelée erupted with ferocious intensity. The first blast threw ash and soot 15 kilometres into the air. The second blast was horizontal, creating a cloud of hot gas (nuée ardente) that travelled at speeds of up to 160 kilometres per hour, at temperatures as high as 1075°C. Even when it hit St. Pierre it would have been over 700°C. Within two minutes 30 000 people were killed and the town was knocked down in the blast (Figure 3.10). Two people survived – the most noteworthy being a prisoner contained in a small room with no windows.

Death would have been quick and from one of three causes:

- the physical impact of the cloud
- inhalation of superhot gases
- burns.

The pyroclastic flow (or nuée ardente – a cloud of super-heated gas-charged ash) at St. Pierre is one of the most tragic examples of how human activity turns a hazard into a disaster.

QUESTIONS

1 Why is Martinique affected by tectonic activity?

2 Describe the main characteristics of a pyroclastic flow (nuée ardente).

3 Briefly describe why people were not evacuated from St. Pierre.

THE MONTSERRAT ERUPTION, 1997

Montserrat is a small island in the Caribbean which has been affected by a number of recent hazards. It is one of the few remaining British colonies. It is a relatively poor country, with much of its economy based on farming and tourism. In 1989 it was hit by Hurricane Hugo. This had a dramatic impact upon tourism and employment. Hotels and restaurants closed down, cruise liners avoided the island and unemployment rose from 7% to 50%. After a slow but steady recovery, Montserrat was affected by another environmental hazard in the mid-1990s, a volcano.

The cause of the volcanic activity on Montserrat is a subduction zone caused by the South American and North American plates plunging under the Caribbean plate (Figure 3.11). Rocks at the edge of the plate melt, deform and rise, forming the Lesser Antilles island arc. The rising magma forms domes (islands). More magma from beneath increases the slope angle, thereby increasing the susceptibility to landslides. When landslides occur on a volcano, its resistance is weakened and new magma can force its way up. Gases in the magma expand rapidly and can send out magma in violent eruptions.

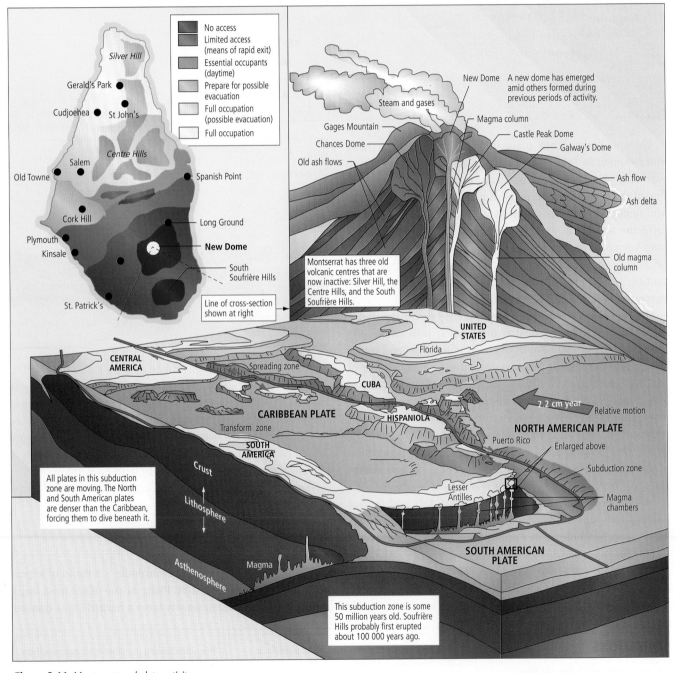

Figure 3.11 *Montserrat and plate activity*
Source: Pierre Mion; Peter Sloss, NOAA; National Geographic Maps

In July 1995, the Soufriere Hills, in the south of the island, after being dormant for nearly 400 years, showed signs of volcanic activity. At first, clouds of ash and steam were given off. In 1996, the volcano finally erupted. It caused mudflows, followed by pyroclastic flows. Part of the dome collapsed, boiling rocks and ash were thrown out and a new dome was created. In June 1997, a further eruption killed nine people and forced the closure of the island's only airport and port. A few months later the capital, Plymouth, was burned to the ground and covered with ash. Fresh eruptions threw out burning rocks, the size of trucks, travelling at speeds of up to 200 kilometres per hour.

The volcanic eruption on Montserrat was small – a minnow compared with the great volcanoes of Krakatoa and Pinatubo. Nevertheless, it has had a severe impact on the people and the island of Montserrat.

Public services and utilities have been moved to the north of the island, away from the agricultural south of the island, at a cost of some £37 million. The largest settlement, Plymouth, with a population of 4000, has been abandoned. This has had a severe impact on Montserrat, as it contained all the government offices, most of the shops and services, such as the market, post office and cinema.

One of the main problems has been the lack of housing for displaced people. For example, up to fifty people have had to share one toilet. Sewage tanks in the temporary shelters were often not emptied for weeks at a time. The risk of contaminated water and the spread of diseases, such as cholera, is greatly intensified by large numbers of people living in overcrowded, unhygienic conditions.

The eruptions have also brought about the partial evacuation of Montserrat itself: over half of its population of 12 000 people have left the island since the volcano awakened in 1995. About 3000 Montserrat refugees have made their way to Antigua and caused a great strain on Antiguan resources. It is not clear how many people are left on Montserrat; in October 1997, the British government stated that there were just 2500 people left on the island whereas the Chief Minister of Montserrat claimed there were over 4000.

Other Caribbean countries provided materials and humanitarian aid to the colony and many other countries provided doctors, nurses, food and medical supplies. The UK, however, was criticised because it appeared unwilling to move quickly or definitively to support the Montserratians. This caused some rioting in Montserrat, protesting at the lack of facilities provided by the Montserrat authorities, and therefore by implication, lack of funding by the UK (Figure 3.12). Critics claimed that the UK was reluctant to accept its full responsibility and that it was hoping that voluntary evacuation would spare the (UK) government the need and cost of moving Montserratians off the island. Nevertheless, the UK has provided some £10 million in aid.

Figure 3.12 *Plymouth, Montserrat, August 1997, after the evacuation*

QUESTIONS

1 Study Figure 3.11 which shows tectonic plates in the Caribbean. Explain why Montserrat is affected by volcanoes.

2 Why do you think the south part of Montserrat was the main agricultural region of the island?

3 What, if any, are the implications of the experience of the Mont Pelée eruption for the island of Montserrat?

4 What should the British government do for the island of Montserrat? Give reasons for your answer.

5 What impact, if any, would political change in the UK have on the government's role in Montserrat? Justify your answer.

6 Assess the following options for people living in the southern part of Montserrat: do nothing; move to the north of the island; take refugee status in Antigua; emigrate to the UK or the USA. For each of these options make two lists, one for the advantages and one for the disadvantages. Which do you think is the best option and why?

NEVADO DEL RUIZ, COLOMBIA, 1985

We have seen the effect of lahars caused by rain in the example of Mount Pinatubo. Here we consider the impact of melting snow and ice on mudflows. The example of Nevado del Ruiz in Colombia, 1985, shows how destructive these lahars can be.

Nevado del Ruiz is a volcano in Colombia which rises to an altitude of 5400 metres and is topped by an ice cap 30 metres thick, covering an area of about 20 square kilometres. In 1984, intermittent small-scale volcanic activity resumed, followed by large-scale activity in November 1985. Scientists monitoring the mountain recorded earthquakes and then a volcanic eruption which threw hot, pyroclastic material onto the ice cap, causing it to melt. Condensing volcanic steam, ice melt and pyroclastic flows combined to form lahars which moved down the mountain engulfing the village of Chinchina, killing over 1800 people and destroying the village (Figure 3.13).

Conditions deteriorated as further eruptions melted more ice, creating larger lahars which were capable of travelling further down the mountain, into the flood plain of the Rio Magdelena. Within an hour of the first volcanic eruption, larger lahars had reached the city of Armero, 45 kilometres away (Figure 3.14). Most of Armero, including 22 000 of its 28 000 residents were crushed and suffocated beneath lahars up to 8 metres thick. The lahar followed the course of least resistance, i.e. the bottom of a valley. Those up the valley slopes, for example at Murillo and Libano, were spared the lahar, those in the valley, for example at Armero and Mariquita, were not so lucky. Images of people trapped in the mud were relayed across the world.

The volcanic eruptions in this case were relatively small. However, the presence of the ice cap made the effects of the eruption disastrous.

QUESTIONS

1 Using Figure 2.3 on page 12, identify the two plates involved in the tectonic activity at Nevado del Ruiz.

2 Explain the main tectonic processes operating at Nevado del Ruiz.

3 What caused the lahars which engulfed Chinchina and Armero?

Figure 3.13 *Nevado del Ruiz – a child is rescued from the lahar at Armero, Colombia*

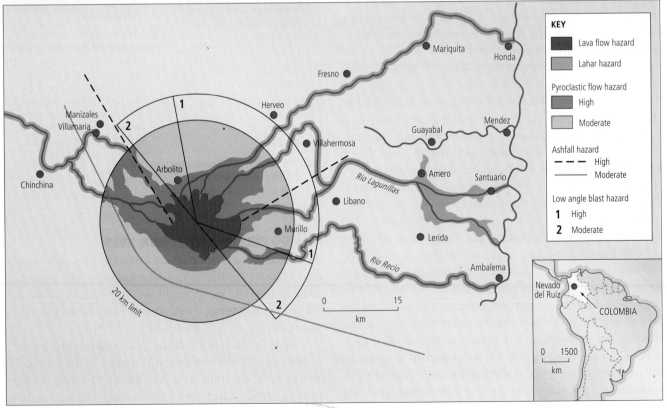

Figure 3.14 *Spread of volcanic hazards from Nevado del Ruiz*
Source: Chester, D., 1993, Volcanoes and society, E. J. Arnold

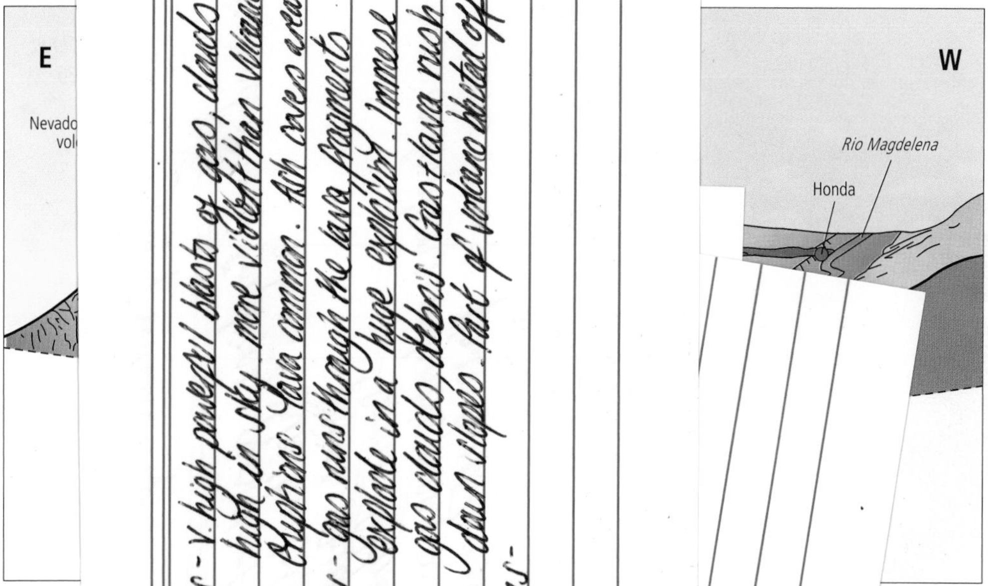

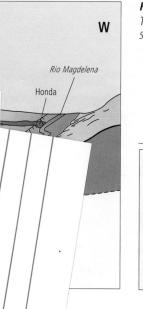

Figure 3.15
The Nevado del Ruiz lahar
Source: US Geological Survey, 1986

Rio Magdelena

Honda

W

E

Nevado
vol

QUESTIONS

1 Why do volcanoes and ice caps sometimes occur in the same place?

2 Study Figure 3.15 which shows the location of Armero. Why do you think so many people lived there?

VOLCA

Camero
It conta
Nyos, f
nearly
August
swept do
25 kilom
ground-h
travelling
1700 pec
life in the area

[Handwritten overlay notes — eruption types:]

Vesuvian eruptions - Very high energy! blasts of gas clouds high in sky, more violent than Vulcanian

Vulcanian eruptions - lava common. Ash cover area

Plinian eruptions - gas rises through the lava fragments. Explode in a huge explosion! Immense gas clouds above. Gas/lava rich

lava slopes. Part of volcano blast off -

carbon dioxide. Because it is heavier and ...ygen, the 50 metre cloud sank, rather than ...ived people and animals of oxygen so that ...nyxiated. The source of the carbon dioxide ...chamber of magma deep beneath Cameroon. ...eaking into and accumulating in Lake Nyos. ...lake had become stratified into layers of ...er near the surface and colder, denser water ...om. The cold, dense water absorbed the carbon ...ich was then held down by the weight of the ...aters.

...ster occurred when the water at the bottom of the ...isturbed. The cause of the disturbance is unclear; it could have been a deep volcanic eruption, an earthquake, a change in water temperature or a climatic event. Whatever the cause, the effect was like champagne exploding from a bottle. Once the overlying pressure was reduced, carbon dioxide escaped into the surrounding area.

It is likely that such a tragedy will happen again. It is believed that only about 66% of the carbon dioxide escaped from the lake and that it has begun to build up again. It may take several decades for the gas cloud to occur again, or maybe even centuries, but the potential for a disaster is there.

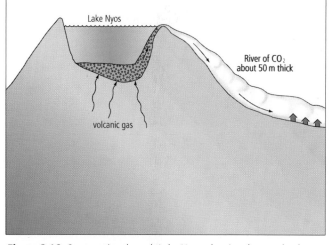

Lake Nyos

River of CO_2
about 50 m thick

volcanic gas

Figure 3.16 Cross section through Lake Nyos, showing the gas cloud
Source: Abbott, P., 1996, Natural disasters, William Brown

QUESTIONS

1 Explain why the disaster at Lake Nyos affected animals but not plants.

2 Cameroon is not close to a tectonic boundary. How do you explain the tectonic hazard in an area that is not close to a known boundary?

Figure 3.17
Livestock killed by the Gas Cloud from Lake Nyos, August 1986

SUMMARY

Volcanic eruptions are among the most dramatic of all processes that occur on earth. We have seen that the forces released in volcanic explosions are indeed awesome. At the same time, more and more people live in areas that are threatened by volcanic hazards. This is partly a result of population growth and the need to inhabit more land, and partly a result of the fertile nature of volcanic soils once they have cooled. Volcanic hazards are diverse: we have seen the effects of lava flows, pyroclastic flows, lahars and gas flows. But we have also seen that human activity is central in the development of a disaster. The case of Mont Pelée showed this clearly, and there are, perhaps, lessons to be learnt on behalf of the islanders of Montserrat. The eruption of Pinatubo illustrated that many deaths may be related, not to the volcanic eruption, but to secondary hazards such as fire and contaminated water.

QUESTIONS

1 Describe, and account for, the distribution of volcanoes as shown on Figure 3.1.
2 Why is volcanic activity becoming an increasingly serious problem?
3 Explain why more people are killed by secondary hazards such as contaminated water and fire, rather than the primary explosion.

BIBLIOGRAPHY AND RECOMMENDED READING

Abbott, P., 1996, *Natural disasters*, William Brown
Bryant, E., 1991, *Natural hazards*, CUP
Ollier, C., 1988, *Volcanoes*, Blackwell
Williams, A., 1997, *Under the volcano: Montserrat*, National Geographic, 192, 1, 58-75

WEB SITES

Alaska volcanoes –
http://www.avo.alaska.edu/
Global assessment of active volcanoes –
http://www.geo.mtu.edu/eos/
Hawaii volcanoes –
http://www.soest.hawaii.edu/hvo/
Mount St. Helens –
http://volcano.und.edu/vwdocs/msh/msh.html
Mount St. Helens blast zone –
http://athena.wednet.edu/curric/land/sthelen/
Mount St. Helens images –
http://vulcan.wr.usgs.gov/
MTU Volcanoes Page –
http://www.geo.mtu.edu/volcanoes/
Volcano World –
http://volcano.und.nodak.edu/

Chapter 4
Landslides and mass movements

So far we have looked at hazards which are relatively unimportant in the UK, although their consequences affect us. In this chapter we focus our attention closer to home and look at the hazards caused by mass movements, in particular landslides (Figure 4.1). We begin the chapter with a discussion and classification of mass movements and then look at their causes. We look at a number of examples of landslides including Hong Kong and the Holbeck Hall Hotel landslip. We finish with a discussion of landslides in the UK.

MASS MOVEMENTS

Mass movements include any large-scale movements of the earth's surface that are not accompanied by a moving agent such as a river, glacier or ocean wave. They include:

- very slow movements, such as soil creep
- fast movements, such as avalanches
- dry movements, such as rock falls
- very fluid movements such as mud flows (Figure 4.2).

A range of slope processes occur which vary in terms of magnitude, frequency and scale. Some, notably rock falls, are large and occur infrequently, whereas others are smaller and more continuous, such as soil creep.

The **types of process** can be classified in a number of different ways:

- speed of movement (Figure 4.3)
- water content
- type of movement: flows, slides, slumps
- material.

Causes of mass movements

The likelihood of a slope failing – the maximum amount of water that can be contained in a slope – can be expressed by its safety factor. This is the relative strength or resistance of the slope, compared with the force which is trying to move it.

Figure 4.1 *Landslide, in the UK – the Aberfan disaster*

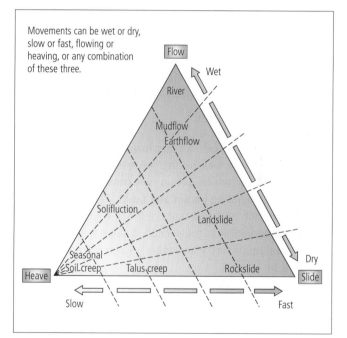

Movements can be wet or dry, slow or fast, flowing or heaving, or any combination of these three.

Figure 4.2 *Carson and Kirby's classification of mass movements*
Source: based on Nagle, G., and Spencer, K., 1997, Advanced geography revision handbook, OUP

Figure 4.3 *Variations in the speed of mass movements*
Source: Nagle, G. and Spencer, K., 1997, Advanced geography revision handbook, OUP

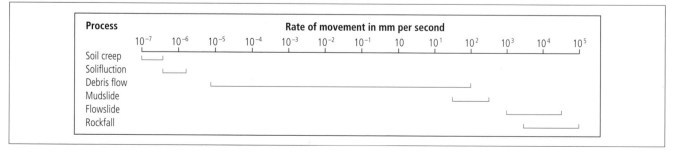

The most important factors that determine movement are:
- **gravity**
- **slope angle**
- **pore pressure** (water pressure in saturated soils, producing a mass movement such as a landslide).

Gravity has two effects: first, it acts to move material downslope (a slide component), second, it sticks particles to a slope (a stick component). The downslope movement is proportional to the weight of the particle and slope angle. When water is present, particles are lubricated and, in some cases, the spaces between the particles are filled; pressure from the water forces the particles apart (pore pressure). Pore pressure greatly increases the ability of the material to move. This factor is of particular importance in movements of wet material on low angle slopes.

Shear strength and shear resistance

Shear strength and **shear resistance** are key ideas in the understanding of mass movements and slope failure. Slope failure is caused by two factors:
- an increase in **shear stress**, that is an increase in the forces attempting to pull a mass downslope
- a reduction in the internal resistance, or **shear strength**, of the slope.

Both can occur at the same time. The factors which can contribute to an increase in shear stress and a reduction in shear strength are shown in Figure 4.4.

Shear stress

Increases in shear stress can be caused by a number of factors. These include weathering processes and changes in water availability which act on weaknesses in the rocks, such as joints, bedding planes and faults. When weathering reduces cohesion and resistance, surface-weathered material may be susceptible to movement on slope angles although the original material was stable. Shear stress may be increased by:
- steepening or undercutting of a slope
- addition of a mass of regolith (mantle rock)
- dumping of mining waste
- sliding from higher up the slope
- vibrational shock
- earthquakes.

Shear strength

Under 'normal' conditions a number of factors keep slopes in position. The downslope movement of slope material is opposed by three main forces:
1 **Friction** varies with the weight of the particle and the slope angle. Friction can be overcome on very gently sloping angles if water is present. For example, solifluction (flowing soil caused by the thawing of once-frozen upper

Factor	Examples
Factors contributing to increased shear stress	
Removal of lateral support through undercutting or slope steepening	Erosion by rivers and glaciers, wave action, faulting, previous rock falls or slides
Removal of underlying support	Undercutting by rivers and waves, subsurface solution, loss of strength by exposure of sediments
Loading of slope	Weight of water, vegetation, accumulation of debris
Lateral pressure	Water in cracks, freezing in cracks, swelling, pressure release
Transient stresses	Earthquakes, movement of trees in wind
Factors contributing to reduced shear strength	
Weathering effects	Disintegration of granular rocks, hydration of clay minerals, solution of cementing minerals in rock or soil
Changes in pore-water	Saturation, softening of material pressure
Changes of structure	Creation of fissures in clays, remoulding of sands and clays
Organic effects	Burrowing of animals, decay of roots

Figure 4.4 *Factors causing increasing shear stress and reduced shear strength*
Source: Summerfield, M., 199l, Global geomorphology, Longman

layers of soil over still-frozen lower layers) can occur on slopes as gentle as 3°.
2 **Cohesive forces** act to bind the particles on the slope. Clay may have high cohesion, but this may be reduced if the water content becomes so high that the clay liquefies and loses its cohesive strength.
3 **Vegetation** binds the soil and thereby stabilises slopes. However, vegetation may allow soil moisture to build up and make landslides more likely.

Water is a vital ingredient in many slope failures. Water can weaken a slope by increasing shear stress and decreasing shear resistance. The weight of a potentially mobile mass is increased by:
- an increase in the volume of water
- heavy or prolonged rain
- rising water tables
- an increase in saturated surface layers.

Moreover, water reduces the cohesion of particles by saturation. Water pressure in saturated soils decreases the frictional strength of the solid material. This weakens the slope. Over time, hazard potential for a particular slope will change. These changes may be gradual: for example, percolation may carry away finer material, or rapid: in Britain, for example, shear stresses increase in winter (Figure 4.5).

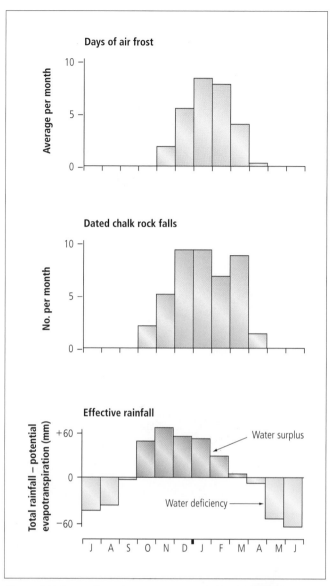

Figure 4.5 *Seasonality and mass movements on the Isle of Thanet*
Source: Collard, R., 1990, The physical geography of landscape, Unwin-Hyman

Figure 4.6 *Running water on slopes causes gully erosion – as here in Australia*

QUESTIONS

1 Define the terms 'shear strength' and 'shear stress'.

2 With the use of examples, explain why mass movements occur.

3 Study Figure 4.5 which shows seasonality of mass movements on the Isle of Thanet.

(i) What is the relationship between the number of days of air frost and the number of rock falls per month?

(ii) How do you account for this relationship?

4 What is meant by the term 'effective rainfall'? Describe and explain how 'effective rainfall' relates to rockfalls.

TYPES OF MASS MOVEMENT

There are a number of processes which result from the impact of running water on slopes (Figure 4.6). **Overland run-off** is the general term given to water flowing over the land's surface. This is sometimes subdivided into two types, **channelled flow** and **unchannelled flow**.

Overland run-off

Surface wash occurs when the soil's infiltration capacity is exceeded. In Britain this commonly occurs in winter as water drains across saturated or frozen ground, following prolonged or heavy downpours or the melting of snow. It is also common in arid and semi-arid regions where particle size limits percolation.

Sheetwash is the unchannelled flow of water over a soil surface. On most slopes, sheetwash breaks into zones of high velocity separated by zones of lower velocity. It is capable of transporting material dislodged by rainsplash (see Figure 4.7, on page 38). Sheetwash occurs in the UK on footpaths and moorlands. For example, during the Lynmouth floods of 1952, sheetwash on the shallow moorland peat created gulleys 6 metres deep. In the semi-arid areas of the south-west USA, sheetwash lowers surfaces by 2-5 millimetres per year compared with 0.01 millimetres per year on vegetated British slopes.

Throughflow refers to water moving down through the soil. It is channelled into natural pipes (covered channels) in the soil. The concentrated areas of high velocity water give it sufficient energy to transport material, and added to its soluble load, may amount to a considerable volume.

Inset 4.1
Rain-splash erosion

Rain-splash erosion accompanies overland run-off. On flat surfaces (1), raindrops compact the soil and dislodge particles equally in all directions. On steep slopes (2), the downward component (a) is more effective than the upward motion (b) due to gravity. Therefore, erosion downslope increases with slope angle (Figure 4.7). On a 5° slope about 60% of the soil movement is downslope. This figure increases to 95% on a 25° slope. The amount of erosion depends upon the rainfall intensity, velocity and raindrop distribution. It is affected by seasonal distribution – rain concentrated in one season causes more erosion than the same amount of rainfall spread over the year. Rain-splash erodes more on slopes of between 33° and 45° and at the start of a rainfall event, such as a shower or storm, before the soil is compacted by the raindrops.

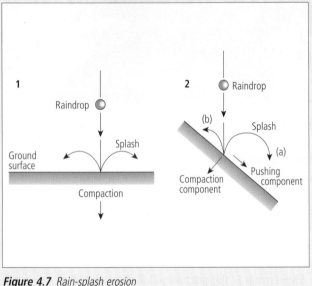

Figure 4.7 *Rain-splash erosion*
Source: Goudie, A., 1993, The nature of the environment, Blackwell

Rock falls

Falls occur on steep slopes (> 70°), especially bare rock faces where joints are exposed. The initial cause of the fall may be weathering, such as freeze-thaw or block disintegration, or erosion prising open lines of weakness. Once the rocks are detached, they fall under the influence of gravity (Figure 4.8 (a)). If the fall is short it produces a relatively straight scree. If it is long, it forms a concave scree. Freeze-thaw on the Marsden Rock, a limestone arch near South Shields, triggered a series of rock falls in the winter of 1995-96 causing the collapse of the arch. A good example of falls and scree is the Wastwater Screes in the Lake District.

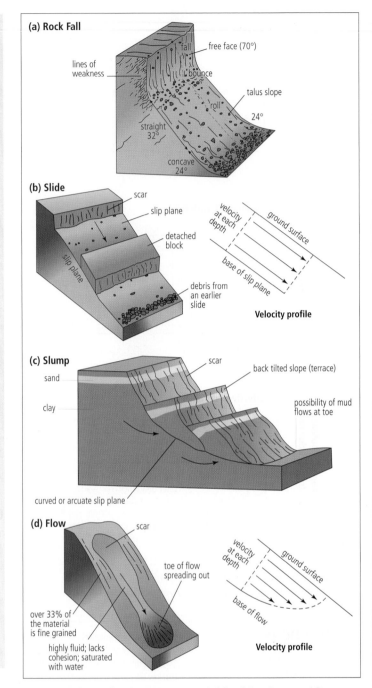

Figure 4.8 *Types of mass movement – rock falls, slides, slumps and flows*
Source: Nagle, G. and Spencer, K., 1997, Advanced geography revision handbook, OUP

Slides

Slides occur when an entire mass of material moves along a **slip plane** (or slide plane). They include:

- rockslides and landslides of any material, rock or regolith
- rotational slides, which produce a series of massive steps or terraces.

Slides commonly occur where there is a combination of weak rocks, steep slopes and active undercutting. Slides are often caused by a change in the water content of a slope or by very cold conditions. As the mass moves along the slip plane, it tends to retain its shape and structure until it hits the bottom of the slope (Figure 4.8 (b)). Slide hazards range from small-scale slides close to roads, to large-scale movements which kill thousands of people, for example, the slide at the Vaiont Dam, Italy, where more than 2000 people died on 9th October 1963, when the dam burst following a massive landslide.

The slip plane can occur at a variety of places:

- at the junction of two layers
- at a fault line
- at a joint
- along a bedding plane
- at the point beneath the surface where the shear stress becomes greater than the shear strength.

Weak rocks, such as clay, have little shear strength and are particularly vulnerable to the development of slip planes. The slip plane is typically a concave curve and as the slide occurs the mass will be rotated backwards.

In 1959, the sixth strongest earthquake to affect the USA occurred in Montana. Close to the epicentre of the earthquake, in the Madison River Valley, a slope of schists and gneiss with slippery mica and clay was supported by a base of dolomite. The earthquake broke the dolomite cleanly. A huge volume of rock, 400 metres high and 1000 metres long, slid into the valley. Eighty million tonnes of material moved in less than a minute! The Madison River was dammed and a lake 60 metres deep and 8 kilometres long was created.

Inset 4.2
The Hong Kong landslides

In Hong Kong in June 1966, rainstorms triggered massive landslides which killed 64 people (Figure 4.9). Over 2500 people were made homeless and a further 8000 were evacuated. Rainfall had been high for the first ten days of June. Over 300 millimetres had fallen, compared with 130 millimetres in a normal year. On 11th and 12th June over 400 millimetres fell; nearly a third of this occurred in just one hour. By 15th June the area had received over 1650 millimetres of rain. Over 700 landslides were recorded in Hong Kong that month.

Vegetation intensified the problem. It held back many of the smaller landslides and allowed larger ones to build up. The main form of landslide was a **washout**. These are large-scale, deep-seated landslides which involve some rotational movement. The washouts were accompanied by the emergence of sub-surface water which helped to erode the slopes below. Other forms of landslides were sheetflows, debris avalanches and rock slides. These three forms of landslide consist of more rock, earth or soil, than a washout, and less water.

Figure 4.9
The Hong Kong landslide, 1966, was caused by the construction of a large tower block on a steep slope – as here

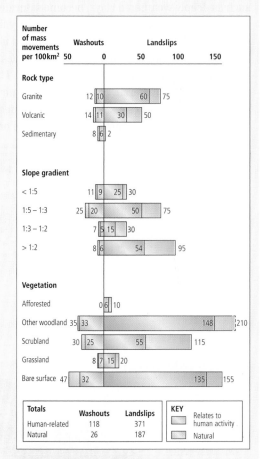

Figure 4.10 Factors affecting landslides in Hong Kong
Source: So, C., 1970, Mass movements associated with the rainstorm of June 1966 in Hong Kong, Transactions of the Institute of British Geographers 53, 55-6

QUESTION

1   Study Figure 4.10 which shows the relationship between mass movements in Hong Kong and rock type, gradient and vegetation. Using the data, describe and explain the relationship between mass movements and (i) rock type, (ii) gradient and (iii) vegetation.

Slumps and flows

Slumps occur on weak rocks, notably clay, and have a rotational movement along a curved slip plane (Figure 4.8 (c), on page 38). Clay absorbs water and becomes saturated and unstable; the clay then flows down along a slip plane. Frequently, slumps occur when the base of a cliff has been undercut and weakened by erosion from the sea, for example, Folkestone Warren in Kent. Human activity can intensify the condition by causing increased pressure on the rocks. This was partly the case at the Holbeck Hall Hotel, Scarborough, where the slow, but inexorable, descent of the hotel down the cliff-face made headline news.

Flows are more continuous and less jerky than slumps, and are more likely to contort the mass into a new form (Figure 4.8 (d), on page 38). Flows occur where fine-grained materials, such as deeply weathered clays, become saturated with water, lose their cohesion and flow downhill as a very fluid mass, for example Aberfan, South Wales. This example is discussed in *Britain's changing environment* in this series. The flow is fastest at the surface and slows with depth. The amount of water, size of the material, cohesion of the material and presence of any weaknesses (faults, slip planes) determine whether the mass movement is a flow, a slide or a slump.

QUESTIONS

1 Explain the terms 'mass movement', 'rotational slide' and 'sheetwash'.

2 Explain how rain-splash erosion takes place.

3 Describe at least **two** ways of classifying mass movements. How useful are these methods of classification?

4 What is meant by the term 'effective rainfall'? Describe and explain how 'effective rainfall' relates to rockfalls.

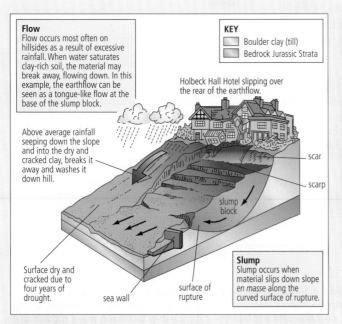

Flow
Flow occurs most often on hillsides as a result of excessive rainfall. When water saturates clay-rich soil, the material may break away, flowing down. In this example, the earthflow can be seen as a tongue-like flow at the base of the slump block.

KEY
☐ Boulder clay (till)
☐ Bedrock Jurassic Strata

Holbeck Hall Hotel slipping over the rear of the earthflow.

Above average rainfall seeping down the slope and into the dry and cracked clay, breaks it away and washes it down hill.

scar

scarp

slump block

Surface dry and cracked due to four years of drought.

sea wall

surface of rupture

Slump
Slump occurs when material slips down slope *en masse* along the curved surface of rupture.

Figure 4.12 *The causes of the Holbeck Hall Hotel landslip*
Source: Yorkshire Post British Geological Survey

Inset 4.3
Holbeck Hall Hotel

On 5th June 1993 a landslip along the upper sections of the boulder clay, on the 60 metre cliffs at Start Bay, Scarborough, caused the destruction of the Holbeck Hall Hotel (Figure 4.11). The hotel had dominated the panorama since its construction in 1883. The coastline between Scarborough and Easington (Spurn Head) is amongst the most rapidly retreating coastal areas in Britain and would cost millions of pounds to protect.

More than a dozen homes in the vicinity of the earthflow are now regarded by estate agents as worthless. The Ministry of Agriculture, which supports coastal protection schemes, issued a statement blaming a succession of droughts for making the area unstable. The boulder clay had become dry and cracked in previous years and then saturated by the rains in spring and early summer. The saturated clay became unstable and slumped along a slip plane thereby causing an earthflow at the base of the slump (Figure 4.12). It is not thought erosion by the sea played a significant role. Little can be done except to let the slip stabilise itself. Geologists believe it will eventually stabilise when it reaches an angle of about 25 degrees. However, the chances of ever building on it again are remote. Once movement has ceased, the options for engineers include improving drainage of the boulder clay, weighting the front edge of the slip to keep it in place or simply allowing nature to take its course.

Figure 4.11 *The Holbeck Hall Hotel landslip*

QUESTIONS

1 **What were (i) the natural causes and (ii) the human factors that led to the Holbeck Hall Hotel slumping in June 1993?**

2 **Why is the coastline between Scarborough and Easington so prone to erosion? Why was erosion by the sea not thought to be a contributory factor?**

3 **Why are the chances of building on it again 'remote'?**

LANDSLIDES IN THE UK

Landslides occur in the UK as a result of a number of inter-acting factors:

- coastal erosion
- geological variations between permeable chalks and over-lying impermeable clays
- frequent storms and a plentiful supply of water
- rising sea level
- past episodes of ground freezing, solifluction (soil flowing under very cold conditions) and cambering (warping or sagging of rocks which overlie clay)
- climatic change
- past sea level changes and river incision
- steep slopes caused by glaciation.

Landslides frequently occur along the UK coastline. Falls, slides and flows are all easily visible along the soft rock coasts of England. In addition, continuing erosion by the sea results in cliff retreat that often exceeds one metre per year. Areas particularly vulnerable include the coasts of Yorkshire, Norfolk, Suffolk, Essex, north Kent, Fairlight in East Sussex and Barton-on-Sea in Hampshire, Portland in west Dorset and south Devon (Figure 4.13).

Some of the most impressive examples are to be found along the coastline of Lyme Regis Bay on the Dorset-Devon boundary.

Inland landslides are often concealed beneath vegetation or have been modified by subsequent erosion and deposi-tion. For example, the Cotswold escarpment is mantled by irregular unstable ground, where limestone has moved over clay causing cambering, leading to landslides and slumps sine the last glacial period.

The inland landslide hazard is problematic for two rea-sons. First, the conditions that determine slope stability can change over time, and second, once a slope has failed, the mass of moved debris represents a danger area more prone to failure than the original slope.

In the past, inland landslides were far more prevalent than today. This was especially true during periglacial times when the climate was changing from cold, tundra conditions to a more equable temperate climate.

Four very important general conclusions about landslides can be drawn:

- landslides in Britain are far more frequent and widely dis-tributed than previously thought
- the impact of landsliding on the economy, through its effects on buildings and engineering projects, is signifi-cant

- the planning profession has limited awareness of the potential significance of the landslide hazard
- available information on landsliding is characterised by marked spatial variability in quantity and quality.

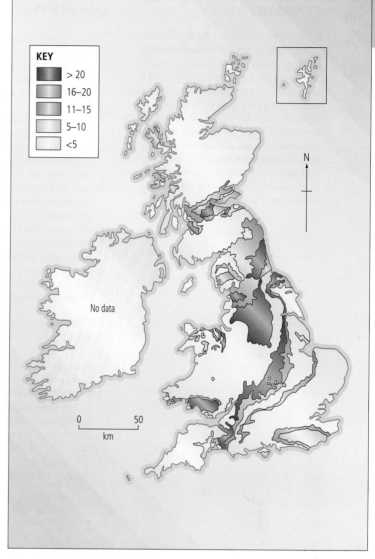

Figure 4.13 *Landslides in the UK*
Source: Goudie, A. and Brunsden, D.,1994, The environment of the British Isles, OUP

QUESTIONS

1 Describe the distribution of landslides as shown in Figure 4.13.

2 How do you account for this distribution?

SUMMARY

In this chapter we have seen the varied nature of mass movements. Many of these are dramatic examples of environmental hazards: it is easy to recognise the destruction and tragedy caused by landslides in Hong Kong and so on. However, we are now becoming more aware of the importance of landslides in the UK – they are not as uncommon as once thought. As with other hazards, the risks from mass movements and landslides are increasing as more and more people live in hazardous areas, as roads are built out of necessity across landslides, and as human activity influences the strength and resistant nature of slopes.

QUESTIONS

1 Study Figure 4.10 (page 39) which provides information on landslides in Hong Kong.
a) What type of mass movement was most common in Hong Kong? What do you think is the difference between a washout and a landslip? Give reasons for your answer.
b) Which type of rock was most affected by (i) washouts and (ii) landslips?
c) What type of mass movement most affected (i) granite and (ii) volcanic rocks? How do you explain these differences?
d) What is the relationship between gradient and mass movement in Hong Kong? Give reasons for your answer.
e) What impact does vegetation have on the type and number of mass movements in Hong Kong? Briefly explain your answer.
f) Briefly discuss the impact of human activity on mass movements. Use the evidence in Figure 4.10 to support your answer.

ESSAYS

1 Explain the effect of (i) climate and (ii) rock type on slope development.
2 Describe how you would carry out a survey to see whether slopes with a stream at their base differ from those without a stream at their base.
3 With the use of examples, explain how mass movements take place.
4 Describe and explain the nature of mass movements in the UK.

BIBLIOGRAPHY AND RECOMMENDED READING

Brunsden, D., and Goudie, A., 1981, *Classic coastal landforms of Dorset*, Geographical Association

Clark, M., and Small, J., 1982, *Slopes and weathering*, CUP

Collard, R., 1988, *The physical geography of landscape*, Unwin Hyman

Dunne, T., and Black, R., 1970, 'Partial area contributions to storm runoff in a small New England watershed', Water Resources Research, 6, 1296-311.

Goudie, A., and Brunsden, D., 1994, *The environment of the British Isles*, OUP

Hilton, K., 1985, *Process and pattern in physical geography*, Unwin Hyman

Perry, A., 1981, *Environmental hazards in the British Isles*, George Allen and Unwin

So, C., 1970, *Mass movements associated with the rainstorm of June 1966 in Hong Kong Transactions of the Institute of British Geographers* 53, 55-6.

Summerfield, M., 1991, *Global geomorphology*, Longman

WEB SITES

Earth Science Index Page –
http://www.iiv.ct.cnr.it/files/volpointers.html
Leicester University –
http://www.geog.le.ac.uk/cti/
MTU Education –
http://www.geo.mtu.edu/
The British Geological Society –
http://192.171.148.40/bgs/home.html

Chapter 5
Rivers and floods

So far we have looked at hazards which are largely geological in origin. As we have seen, however, associated or secondary disasters, such as fire, flooding and subsidence, often follow. In this chapter we concentrate on rivers and flooding (inundation). Not all types of flood are discussed here – for example coastal flooding and glacial flooding are discussed in chapters 6 and 7. We begin by looking at the reasons why people live on flood plains, the factors controlling floods, flood hydrographs and options for managing a flood hazard. Our examples include floods in Europe in the mid-1990s, flooding on the River Thames, and a case study on the effects of land use changes and population pressure on the flood hazard in Trinidad and Tobago.

WATER AND SEDIMENT DISCHARGE

Discharge of water and sediment in rivers varies greatly in space and time. In flood conditions the river channel is unable to contain the discharge, so water and sediment spill onto, and move across, adjacent surfaces. Where these surfaces are adjacent to perennial rivers, they are usually called **alluvial flood plains**. In areas where river flow is intermittent, floods often spread across the surfaces to create **alluvial fans**.

Rivers and river valleys are very attractive to people for a variety of reasons. These include:

- a source of drinking water
- a source of fertile silt for agriculture
- a source of power
- for fishing
- for recreation
- a line of communication and navigation.

However, a severe flood can be extremely dangerous to people and their possessions, and many settlements although built in a river valley, are located in order to reduce the risk of flooding. For example, around Oxford much of the flood plain of the Thames and the Cherwell rivers has not been built upon; it has been left for farming and for recreational space, with housing and industry on the higher ground (Figure 5.1).

FLOOD PLAINS AND ALLUVIAL FANS

Flood plains may be defined in various ways: to the geomorphologist, the area is characterised by a distinctive suite of landforms and deposits; to the hydrologist, it is an area subject to floods of particular magnitudes and frequencies

Figure 5.1 *Oxford's flood plain and land use zoning*

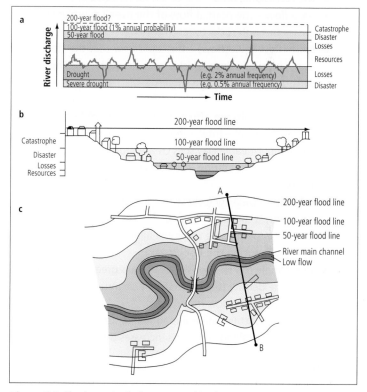

Figure 5.2 *Flood magnitude, frequency and land use*
Source: Hewitt, K., 1997, Regions of risk, Longman

(Figure 5.2); and to planners and lawyers it may be an area subject to certain building and insurance restrictions. Figure 5.2 shows the relationship between flood magnitude, frequency, land use and economic loss. In diagram (a) we see that most flows are contained within normal operating levels. Disasters are caused by extremes of floods or drought and catastrophes are caused under very extreme conditions. The distinction between a disaster and a catastrophe, in the case of floods, is that the latter has a higher magnitude but a lower frequency.

Inset 5.1
Flood hydrographs

A flood hydrograph shows how a storm affects a stream or river over a short period, such as a few hours, or up to a few days. It shows a number of features which vary from stream to stream. The key features are:

- **discharge** – the amount (volume) of water passing a point over a given length of time, e.g. litres per second or cubic metres per second (cumecs)
- **peak flow** – the greatest discharge of the stream
- **time lag** – the difference in time between the peak of the storm and the peak of the flood
- the **rising limb** – the rising floodwater
- the **recessional limb** – the declining floodwater
- **base flow** – the normal flow of the river, i.e. water that passes through rocks to reach the river
- **storm flow (quickflow)** – the rapid flow that the storm creates – it usually flows quickly over the surface of the surrounding area to the stream.

Flood hydrographs are affected by a number of factors:
- climate (rainfall – total, intensity, seasonality)
- soils (impermeable clay soils create more flooding)
- vegetation (vegetation intercepts rainfall and so flooding is less likely)
- infiltration capacity (soils with a low infiltration capacity cause much overland run-off)
- rock type (permeable rocks will allow water to infiltrate, thereby reducing the flood peak)
- slope angle (on steeper slopes there is greater run-off)
- drainage density (the more stream channels there are, the more water can flow into rivers)
- human impact (creating impermeable surfaces and additional drainage channels increases the risk of flooding).

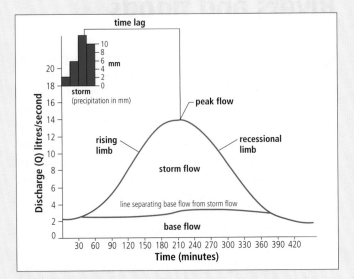

Figure 5.3 *A storm hydrograph*
Source: Nagle, G. and Spencer, K., 1997, Skills and techniques in geography, Stanley Thornes

Urban hydrographs usually differ from rural hydrographs. They have:
- a shorter time lag
- a steeper rising limb
- a higher peak flow
- a steeper recessional limb.

This is because there are more impermeable surfaces in urban areas (roofs, pavements, roads, buildings) as well as more drainage channels (gutters, drains, sewers).

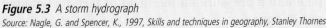

Figure 5.4 *Flood hydrograph – changes in discharge in an urban stream*
Source: Nagle, G. and Spencer, K., 1997, Skills and techniques in geography, Stanley Thornes

Time (mins)	0	30	60	90	120	150	180	210	240	270	300	330	360	390	420
Discharge	4.4	8.0	20.0	35.0	44.0	36.0	26.0	18.4	14.0	9.6	7.4	6.4	5.8	5.6	4.0

QUESTIONS

1 Figure 5.3 shows a storm hydrograph from a stream in a rural area. The data in Figure 5.4 shows how the discharge in a nearby urban stream changed after the same storm. Plot the data from Figure 5.4 onto a copy of the graph in Figure 5.3 to show:

a) the peak flow and time lag in the urban hydrograph
b) how the rising limb and recessional limbs in the new hydrograph compare with the original (rural) one.
2 Explain the differences between rural and urban hydrographs, with reference to the increase in impermeable surfaces (pavements, roads, buildings, etc.) and number of drainage channels (sewers, gutters, drains, ditches, streams).

Alluvial fans are fairly common landforms in arid and semi-arid areas and they are usually found where seasonal or ephemeral flows of water from mountains spread out on to adjacent plains, in the form of many channels crossing a cone-shaped area of silt. Flooding on alluvial fans occurs in two principal locations:

- along the margins of the main water supply channels
- in the depositional zones beyond the end of the water supply channels.

There are several problems associated with floods on alluvial fans:

- as the flow of water on the fans is seasonal, the likelihood of flood is often minimised or ignored
- the water channels can change – for example, when a channel becomes blocked with debris – and so hazard areas may change.

The problem of flooding in dryland areas is considered in more depth in Chapter 9, Drought and desertification.

FACTORS AFFECTING FLOODING

The impact of flooding on human activity is affected by:

- the frequency of flooding
- peak flow (magnitude)
- the velocity of flow
- the rate of a discharge – increase or decline
- total flood run-off volume (the discharge above base flow, i.e. 'normal' or pre-flood level of the river)
- the depth of flood water
- the area inundated
- the duration of inundation
- the lag time
- the sediment load of the flood
- time of year (seasonality).

A number of factors, such as climate and human activity, control these characteristics. Heavy snowfalls and melting are commonly responsible for spring floods in middle and high latitudes. Meltwater in a snowfield freezes during the winter, reducing the amount of water that can percolate through the underlying rocks, so meltwater travels overland into the drainage system. Similarly, excessive precipitation, such as that associated with depressions, hurricanes, and thunderstorms, leads to flooding. Rainfall also varies in terms of duration, intensity, total and areal extent. A classic example of the effect of an intense storm, following a period of heavy rain is the Lynmouth flood of 1952 (Inset 5.2, page 46).

Human activity tends to increase run-off. In Figure 5.5 a hydrograph for a single storm is shown for an area before and after urbanisation. Urbanisation increases the area of impermeable surface in the catchment – houses, roads, paths and pavements produce rapid run-off by feeding water directly into the drainage system. Drains and sewers reduce

lag time, so the flood peak increases and the rising and recessional limbs steepen. In general, the greater the area served by sewers and the greater the impervious area, the greater will be the ratio of peak discharge to discharge before urbanisation.

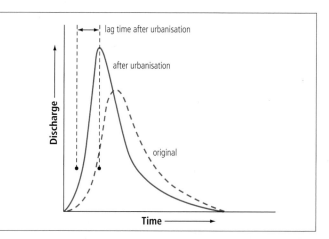

Figure 5.5 *Hydrograph showing discharge before and after urbanisation*
Source: Nagle, G, 1998, Geography through diagrams, OUP

Discharge	Sediment load
Urbanisation	+ 0/+
Reservoir development	0/ − −
Mining	0 +
Deforestation	+ +
0 No change + Increase − Decrease	

Figure 5.6 *Human activities and the effect on flooding*

The building of dams also affects run-off (Figure 5.6). There has been a rapid increase in the pace of dam construction with up to two dams completed worldwide every day. The dams bring a wide range of environmental consequences – sometimes beneficial, at others, detrimental. These include:

- downstream decreases in the sediment load, for example the River Nile in Egypt now only carries two million tonnes of sediment downstream of the Aswan Dam – before the dam was built it carried around 130 million tonnes annually
- clear water erosion (increased rates of erosion by water free of sediment), for example, downstream of the Hoover Dam there is erosion for 130 kilometres reaching depths of seven metres
- lower river discharge leads to narrowing of channels, e.g. the North Platte river, Nebraska, reduced in size at one point, from 735 metres to 110 metres between 1900 and 1970
- flood magnitudes decrease by as much as 75%.

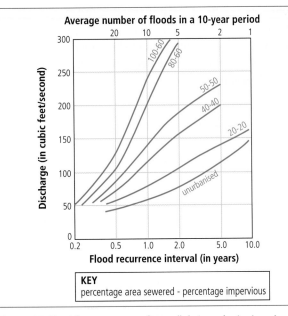

Figure 5.7 *Flood frequency curves for small drainage basins in various stages of urbanisation*
Source: Leopold, L. B., Hydrology for urban planning, US geological survey circular 554, 1968

Inset 5.2
Lynmouth flood disaster, August 1952

On August 15th 1952, the River Lyn overflowed its banks, flooding the town of Lynmouth, with disastrous results: 34 people died; 1000 people were made homeless; 90 houses/hotels were destroyed; 130 cars and 19 boats were lost; cost £10 million (1952 prices).

The factors affecting the flood were:
- intense rain (230 millimetres in 14 hours – 10 mm per 24 hours is the average during a rainfall event)
- high antecedent precipitation (in the previous two weeks)
- small catchment area; water quickly collected in river
- narrow, steep sided valley
- river channel made narrower due to building of bridges, tourist accommodation and amenities
- peak discharge was so great (511 m³/s) that only twice in the last century has it been exceeded by the River Thames (100 times the catchment area)
- bridges trapped boulders (up to seven tonnes in weight) and trees, causing temporary dams which later broke, causing a wave 12 metres high to travel downstream at speeds estimated at thirty kilometres/hour; altogether 100 000 tonnes of boulders moved
- no recording or early warning system.

Mining activities affect river flooding. For example, hydraulic mining for gold between 1855 and 1883 led to long-term changes on the Sacramento River (California). Waste material was dumped in the river. This led to an increase in the transported load of the river, and greater erosion downstream due to the river carrying more, and larger, rocks. The effects included increased flooding, reduction in river's navigable channels as well as erosion of farmland. In 1884, court action prohibited further dumping of spoil. However, it took nearly 100 years for all the debris to reach San Francisco, where it was dropped on the river bed.

QUESTIONS

1 Using the data shown in Figure 5.7, describe and explain the changes that occur in the magnitude and frequency of flood discharge as urbanisation increases.

2 What were some of the natural features of the area drained by the River Lyn which made Lynmouth vulnerable to a possible flood?

3 How had the development of Lynmouth increased the risk of damage from flooding?

4 What extreme conditions in 1952 resulted in the worst flood for over 200 years in Lynmouth?

PERCEPTION AND RESPONSE

Perception of flooding is in part related to some or all of the physical characteristics of the hazard itself, such as the magnitude and the frequency of the flood. The responses to flooding are a product of money, knowledge, perception, technology and the characteristics of the flood and the success of the prediction. Responses include:
- bearing the loss
- emergency action
- flood proofing
- land-use zoning
- flood insurance
- flood control.

Emergency action involves the removal of people and property and provision of various flood-fighting techniques, such as sandbag defences. These depend on the efficiency of flood-forecasting techniques and the amount of time available to warn people and clear the area. Emergency action is generally most effective where flood duration is short, where velocity is low and where frequency of flooding is high.

Flood-proofing measures designed to reduce damage to structures and goods within the hazard zones can take many forms, such as control of seepage by sealing walls and sewer adjustment by the use of valves.

The regulation of land use in flood-hazard zones and the maintenance of adequate floodways are further ways of limiting the damage. However, there are practical problems related to land-use zoning, including the difficulty of esti-

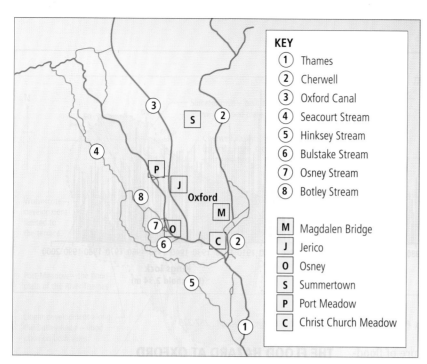

KEY
1. Thames
2. Cherwell
3. Oxford Canal
4. Seacourt Stream
5. Hinksey Stream
6. Bulstake Stream
7. Osney Stream
8. Botley Stream

M Magdalen Bridge
J Jerico
O Osney
S Summertown
P Port Meadow
C Christ Church Meadow

Figure 5.8 *Flood relief channels around Oxford are used to take some of the water from the main channel of the Thames at times of flood*
Source: Elsom, D., 1987, Taming the rivers of Oxford, Witney Press

mating the potential damage to and possible use of the land, with protection works giving a false sense of security. Flood insurance is widely seen as a good alternative to flood plain management but its lack of availability in many poor communities makes it of limited use.

By far the most effective measures to modify flooding are by providing flood relief channels (Figure 5.8) and modifications to the river channels or banks to enable the river to carry greater discharges (Figure 5.9).

Other methods include levees (riverside embankments), removal of boulders from river beds to river banks (reducing channel roughness and protecting banks from erosion), and raising the level of the flood plain. Flood abatement (through the alteration of land use within a catchment area) tackles the problem by slowing down the rate at which water from storms reaches the river channel. There are several ways of achieving this:

- afforestation – increasing interception and evapotranspiration
- terracing of farm land, contour ploughing and strip cultivation – enabling overland flow to be controlled.

CHANGING FLOOD PATTERNS ON THE RIVER THAMES

Flooding in Britain is very diverse. Some records show little change over the last century, whereas others suggest an increase in the amount of flooding in winter (related to higher winter rainfall). Some rainfall records suggest an increasingly seasonal rainfall pattern, others point to higher rainfall (especially in northern areas).

The River Thames has daily records which date back to 1883 – lock keepers are required to make three-hourly records and this provides a large amount of data for the course of the Thames (Figure 5.10, page 48). A common pattern of flood levels across southern England is apparent – a greater number of flood peaks before 1940. The highest flood peaks were in 1894, followed by 1947. Floods on the Thames are predominantly winter phenomena. Most flooding is caused by high intensity rainfall and high levels of antecedent rainfall. Summer thunderstorms have little impact on the Thames because they are localised events.

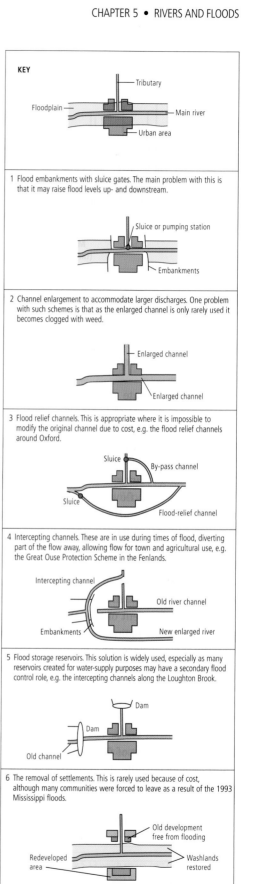

KEY

1 Flood embankments with sluice gates. The main problem with this is that it may raise flood levels up- and downstream.

2 Channel enlargement to accommodate larger discharges. One problem with such schemes is that as the enlarged channel is only rarely used it becomes clogged with weed.

3 Flood relief channels. This is appropriate where it is impossible to modify the original channel due to cost, e.g. the flood relief channels around Oxford.

4 Intercepting channels. These are in use during times of flood, diverting part of the flow away, allowing flow for town and agricultural use, e.g. the Great Ouse Protection Scheme in the Fenlands.

5 Flood storage reservoirs. This solution is widely used, especially as many reservoirs created for water-supply purposes may have a secondary flood control role, e.g. the intercepting channels along the Loughton Brook.

6 The removal of settlements. This is rarely used because of cost, although many communities were forced to leave as a result of the 1993 Mississippi floods.

Figure 5.9 *Possible solutions to flooding*
Source: Smith, K. and Tobin, G., 1979, Human adjustment to flood hazard, Longman

FLOODING IN THE NETHERLANDS, 1995

In January 1995 over 70 000 residents in the eastern Netherlands were urged to leave their homes as rising flood-waters threatened a potential disaster. The evacuation was the largest in the Netherlands since the storm surge of 1953. So many people responded to the warning that the roads were jammed. This followed the evacuation of nearly 10 000 people from the town of Maastricht after the River Maas flooded along 140 kilometres of its length.

Over 40 years earlier, in February 1953, a combination of high tides and severe storms caused the North Sea dikes to be breached. 1835 people drowned and thousands of livestock were killed. 300 000 people were made homeless as roads, houses, dikes and communication links were destroyed.

Despite the Dutch government's annual budget of £280 million for dike maintenance, repair and flood control, nearly a quarter of a million people were evacuated from their homes as rising flood waters affected the lower parts of the Rhine and the Maas in 1995. Almost a third of a million livestock were affected and the Netherlands' highly intensive market gardening, horticulture and dairy industries were seriously disrupted by the floods.

The government subsequently announced a £1 billion plan to strengthen and repair 600 kilometres of river dikes. In order to protect valuable farmland, larger, wider and straighter river dikes are needed. But enlarging the dikes requires nearby houses, trees, roads and barns to be removed, as house foundations and tree roots allow water to percolate the dike. Many Dutch residents have become increasingly concerned about the environmental costs of protecting sea and river dikes.

The January 1995 floods resulted from a period of extremely wet weather in northern Europe. The wet weather was due to a series of depressions (areas of low pressure) carrying warm, moist air from the north Atlantic. These depressions are normally blocked by cold anticyclones (areas of high pressure), which force the depressions to pass north of the UK and the Netherlands. In the absence of these blocking anticyclones, the depressions swept across Europe in quick succession.

QUESTIONS

1 Describe the weather conditions that were experienced over Europe in January 1995 during the Dutch floods (Figure 5.14).

2 Why is straightening of the river dikes considered a part of flood control? Explain your answer.

FLOODING IN EASTERN AND CENTRAL EUROPE, 1997

The floods in eastern and central Europe in July 1997 were one of the continent's worst natural disasters of this century – in Poland over sixty people were killed and in the Czech Republic, fifty people. The floods were the result of two unusually heavy periods of rain in July. In the first bout, which started on 4th July, more rain fell in five days than some parts of western Europe would expect in a year. The heavy rainfall resulted from a virtually stationary area of low pressure which produced nearly continuous rain. In addition, the area suffered heavy downpours from thunderstorms caused by the heat of the ground pushing air upwards. This weather is consistent with the likely impact of global warming.

In Germany, about 1.5 million sandbags were used to strengthen the banks of the Oder and Neisse rivers. The low lying areas along these rivers are protected by dikes, however some of these are nearly 400 years old and are vulnerable to cracking. Increasing numbers of long cracks

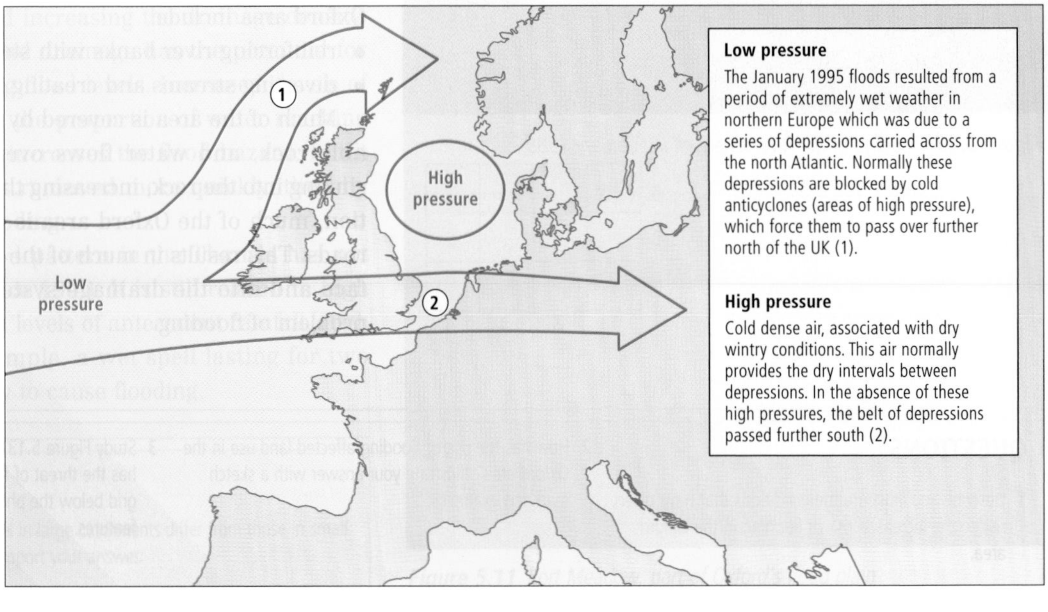

Figure 5.14 Weather conditions over Europe, January 1995
Source: based on The Guardian, 31 January 1995

Low pressure
The January 1995 floods resulted from a period of extremely wet weather in northern Europe which was due to a series of depressions carried across from the north Atlantic. Normally these depressions are blocked by cold anticyclones (areas of high pressure), which force them to pass over further north of the UK (1).

High pressure
Cold dense air, associated with dry wintry conditions. This air normally provides the dry intervals between depressions. In the absence of these high pressures, the belt of depressions passed further south (2).

Figure 5.15 Flooding at Frankfurt, on the River Oder, Germany in July 1997

emerged in dikes in Oderbruch, a low-lying area of flood plain north of Frankfurt, along the river Oder, which was reclaimed in the eighteenth century. Helicopters dumped five-tonne sacks of sand at the foot of the dike near Hohenwutzen, on the Oder, to reinforce two areas where foundations had cracked under the weight of two weeks of floods.

The River Oder burst through a dike on its west bank at Brieskow-Finkenheerd, a few kilometres south of Frankfurt. Army helicopters dropped giant sandbags into the gap in vain. The hole in the riverside defences rapidly widened to 250 metres, and water flooded at a rate of 500 cubic metres per second into a surrounding low-lying area of sixty square kilometres. The authorities ordered the evacuation of more than 2000 people from nearby villages, but many refused to move for fear of looting.

In addition, there were other unexpected hazards. Soldiers building a back-up dike along the River Oder had to stop work temporarily when unexploded World War II bombs were discovered in a gravel pit – workers digging up gravel found seven small German-made bombs, a mine and several grenades in the pit near Reitwein, a village in the Oderbruch flood plain.

In Romania, flooding and harsh weather killed fifteen people in the far northwest and severe storms caused flooding and landslides in the south of the country. A landslide threatened to destroy twenty houses in the county of Prahova. The floods submerged some 1000 homes in the town of Breaza, 160 kilometres north of Bucharest, as well as dozens of houses in villages across the country. Rains also disrupted road and railway traffic between the cities of Ploiesti and Brasov.

In the Czech Republic and Poland the total cost of flood damage was put at more than US$750 million. Experts in the insurance industry say many homeowners and businesses were not insured, since cover for flood damage is not included automatically in policies sold in these countries, making the effects of the disaster all the greater. In the Czech Republic, where floods affected one-third of the country, Czech infrastructure and communications suffered at least US$180 million in damage. Fifteen bridges and 946 kilometres of railway track were destroyed; and more than 135 000 animals were drowned. An estimated 45 000 Polish homes suffered severe damage, and at its peak water covered 550 000 hectares.

QUESTIONS

1 What were the causes of the widespread flooding in eastern and central Europe during 1997?

2 Briefly explain **two** factors which increased the risk of hazard. Use examples to support your answer.

3 Why were so few people covered by insurance? Why should this be a problem?

Case study: **Developing the Santa Cruz catchment, Trinidad**

Figure 5.16 The Santa Cruz catchment, Trinidad

Santa Cruz is a lush, mountainous area near Port of Spain in the north west of the island of Trinidad in the Caribbean Windward Islands (Figure 5.16).

Conditions in the Santa Cruz catchment show certain similarities to the catchments of the East and West Lyn:

- the catchment area is small, just 53.9 square kilometres
- mean annual rainfall is high, 1700 millimetres, largely between June and December (the dry season is between January and May)
- mean stream flow is 0.6 cumecs
- range of elevation is 680 metres
- 62% of slopes are >30% (i.e. very steep)
- natural forest covers 50% of the area
- since 1964 the dry season has become drier.

Agriculture, consisting of cocoa, fruit and vegetables, is mostly in the valley bottoms. Some irrigation for vegetable growing takes place on the Aranguez Estate; this irrigation makes use of the

Figure 5.17 Environmental degradation in the Santa Cruz catchment

gravel aquifer which also supplies most of the domestic water supply for the catchment. The River Caroni is vital for dry season supplies, although it is heavily polluted by industrial waste. Consequently, aquifers are of increasing importance as a source of water, and there has been a gradual increase in abstraction since 1964.

There has been much environmental degradation in the Santa Cruz

catchment (Figure 5.16), caused by a number of interrelated factors:

- deforestation – 265 hectares have been cut down since 1969
- urbanisation – 250 hectares have been lost with a consequent rise in run-off on the flatter areas
- quarrying
- squatter settlements on steep slopes
- a lack of soil and water conservation
- slash and burn agriculture leading to forest fires
- pollution of water courses
- lack of law enforcement relating to environmental standards.

The effects of degradation are very varied. The loss of forest has led to a decline in biodiversity – a loss of wildlife and ecology. Run-off has increased dramatically – run-off on grass is 200-300 times greater than if the same area were covered by forest. There has been a marked increase in gully and sheet erosion, and the number of landslides in the area has increased rapidly. Up to 660 000 cubic metres of soil per year are lost from the catchment.

US$ – 1993	
Soil and water conservation	50
Reforestation (100 ha)	375
Aranguez Estate (through drainage improvement)	237
River improvement in lower catchment	1750
Flood storage	350
River improvement in middle and upper catchments	514
Drilling two wells	350
Research and demonstration	63
Extension training in schools	130
Recreation park	20
Nature trails	30
Total cost	3866

The flood hazard has increased. In 1969, the 25-year flood on the River Caroni (i.e. that which would be expected to occur once every 25 years) was 144 cumecs; by 1992 it had risen to 160 cumecs. Between 1969 and 1986 the annual run-off increased from 300 millimetres to 450 millimetres. In addition, the time lag of the floods has decreased. Since 1971 flooding has been

Figure 5.18 Protection measures in the Santa Cruz catchment

Deforestation	US$36 000/ha annually (incremental loss)
Urbanisation	US$52 000/ha annually (incremental loss)

Figure 5.19 Costs from degradation in the Santa Cruz catchment, e.g. flood damage, dredging

more instantaneous (especially in the 'dry season' floods).

The quality of the River Caroni has worsened since 1969. Water quality decreases downstream and water used for irrigation has a faecal count above that of WHO recommended standards. Increased siltation has led to an increase in mangroves in the Caroni swamp, reducing the amount of open water and upsetting the delicate local ecology. This, in turn, has had an adverse impact on the local fisheries industry. The sediment

at the mouth of the Caroni river crosses shipping lanes which therefore have to be dredged every year – it is a problem which continues to increase.

The strategy for the Santa Cruz catchment must take into account long-term safety and environmental considerations, such as the sustainable use of scarce resources by a rapidly growing population, as well as economic growth. The costs involved are shown in Figures 5.18 and 5.19.

QUESTIONS

1 Describe two contrasting reasons why flooding and erosion have increased in the Santa Cruz catchment.

2 What are the effects of degradation on the physical and economic environment of the Santa Cruz catchment?

SUMMARY

We have seen how river floods are affected by a number of factors. These include physical factors such as the nature and intensity of rainfall, catchment size and shape, and geology. In addition, we have seen how human activity has increased the risk of flooding. This is not just related to urbanisation but includes dam building, mining and residence in unsafe areas. We have also seen that there are a number of ways in which people can live with a flood hazard. These range from simple acceptance to highly technical flood protection schemes.

QUESTIONS

1 Describe the conditions that cause floods.
2 Discuss the methods used to alleviate the risk of flooding. How else could the hazard be 'treated'?
3 With the use of examples, describe and explain the most effective ways of living with the flood hazard.
4 In what ways does the flood hazard in a developing country differ from that in a developed country?

Extended (Project) work

Contact your local Environment Agency or Meteorological Office. Ask them for details relating to flooding in your area. Find out:
● during which months most floods occur
● what size the peak flows are
● if there is a difference between summer and winter peaks
● if there are any trends in the flood peak and frequency over time.

Study the land use of an urban area near you.
● How has human activity altered the rivers and hydrology of the area?
● How have rivers affected land use in your chosen area?

At school, or home, construct a flood hydrograph for an individual storm. To measure rainfall you will need a rain gauge and you should record rainfall every hour or half-hour. To measure discharge collect and measure water coming down a gutter pipe (you may have to find a gutter pipe that you can modify (Figure 5.25)). Plot the flood hydrograph for your storm.

BIBLIOGRAPHY AND RECOMMENDED READING

Crooks, S., 1994, *Changing flood peak levels on the River Thames*, Proc. Instn. Civ. Engrs. Wat., Marit. & Energy, 106, Sept., 267-279.
Elsom, D., 1987, *Taming the rivers of Oxford*, Witney Press
Goudie, A., 1993, *The nature of the environment*, Blackwell
Smith, D. and Stopp, P., 1978, *The river basin*, Cambridge
Ward, R., 1978, *Floods*, Macmillan

WEB SITES

FEMA fact sheet: floods and flash floods – http://www.fema.gov/fema/floodf.html
Floods – http://www.yahoo.com/Science/Earth_Sciences/Meteorology/Weather_phenomena/Floods/
Hydrology related internet resources – http://terrassa.pnl.gov:2080/EESC/resourcelist/hydrology.html

Chapter 6
Coastal hazards

In this chapter we examine hazards in coastal areas. The hazards are wide ranging and include global warming, storm surges, flooding, tsunami, and coastal erosion (Figure 6.1). We begin with an overview of global warming and look at the impact it could have on the UK and on lowlands, such as the Maldives (a group of coral islands in the Indian Ocean). We study the nature of storm surges and look at case studies from the UK and Bangladesh. Tsunamis rank as the most destructive waves – here we look at their impact on Japan. Finally, we look at coastal erosion in the UK and examine how human activity has both increased the risk of erosion and also devised ways to reduce the impact of flooding.

GLOBAL WARMING

'Each tick of the clock could be time lost in saving some thirty small islands from drowning in a sea of rising tides.' Maumoon Abdul Gayoom, President of the Maldives, warned delegates at the Berlin Conference on Environmental Change in 1995.

The 'greenhouse effect' refers to the increase in the level of carbon dioxide (CO_2) and other 'greenhouse gases' in the atmosphere. Since 1850 the CO_2 level in the atmosphere has increased from 220 ppm to 360 ppm (Figure 6.3). The

Figure 6.1 Low-lying island at risk from rising sea levels, saline intrusions and an increase in storm frequency and intensity

increasing concentrations of greenhouse gases result from human activities, such as emissions from cars and the use of spray cans containing chlorofluorocarbons (CFCs). CO_2 allows incoming short-wave radiation to pass through the earth's atmosphere, but blocks out-going long-wave radiation (Figure 6.2). This process traps heat which would otherwise escape from the lower atmosphere.

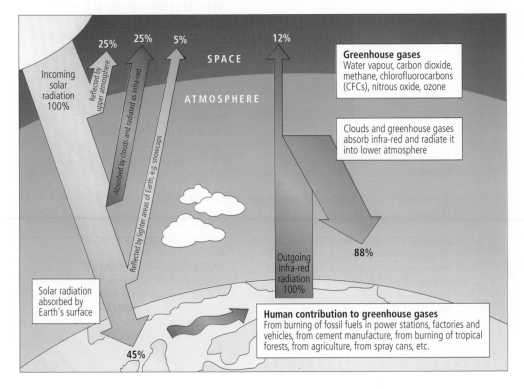

Figure 6.2 Increasing global temperatures and levels of atmospheric CO_2
Source: Robinson, A., 1993, Earthshock, Thames and Hudson

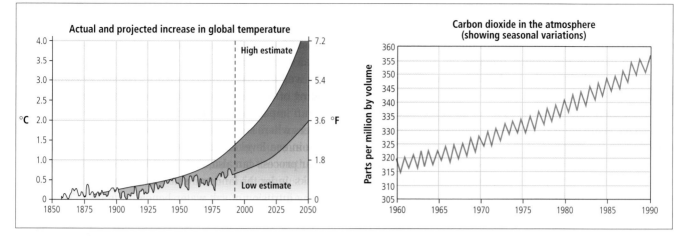

Figure 6.3 *The greenhouse effect*
Source: Robinson, A., 1993, Earthshock, Thames and Hudson

- Temperatures are expected to rise between 1.5°C and 4.5°C during the twenty-first century.

- Mean sea level is rising at a rate of 3 millimetres per day. Flooding of low lying areas will be accompanied by an increase in the frequency and intensity of storms. The cause of rising sea levels is global warming. This also means that there is more energy in the atmosphere, which means that storms may be more intense, causing more erosion. As temperatures continue to rise, the frequency of these storms will increase.

- The results of the greenhouse effect will vary from place to place. Some areas will become warmer, especially polar and sub-polar areas – parts of Alaska are 2°C warmer now than in 1890, and coastal Antarctica has warmed by over 2.5°C since 1945, causing ice sheets to disintegrate; the James Ross Island became disconnected from Antarctica in 1995, the first time in recorded history.

- Warming will be greater over land than oceans.

- Ocean currents and salinity levels will be changed.

- Africa and South America will be warmed but China will not because of its large level of sulphate pollution.

- Acid rain will increase.

- Increased snowfalls will affect Antarctica.

Figure 6.4 *Some predicted effects of increased levels of CO_2*

As a result of the heat being trapped, the earth's surface and lower atmosphere are expected to warm (Figure 6.4). This warming is likely to continue, even if emissions of greenhouse gases were to cease, because of past increases in greenhouse gases and time lags in the climatic system. One of the major consequences of this warming may be a world wide rise in the mean sea level. In addition, there may be an increase in the frequency and intensity of coastal storms. The earth's temperature has risen by over 0.5°C since 1850, raising sea levels as a result of thermal expansion and melting of the polar ice caps. (The sea is expanding at a rate of 0.4 mm per year as a result of higher tempera-

tures.) The UN Intergovernmental Panel on Climatic Change predicts that sea levels could rise by as much as 1 metre by the year 2100. Over the past century, the mean sea level is estimated to have risen by around 10 to 15 centimetres and the rate of rise is likely to increase over the next hundred years. Estimates of the likely effects of global warming suggest additional rises in the sea level of perhaps 10 to 30 centimetres by 2030.

The impact of the greenhouse effect over the next century is as yet unclear; there are many conflicting interests and not all countries are willing to attempt to reduce their emissions of CO_2.

However, it is not just the greenhouse effect that can cause a rise in sea levels: the extraction of oil and groundwater, subsidence, tectonic and isostatic movements are all contributing factors. Moreover, scientists still do not fully understand the mechanics of the atmosphere: CO_2 is only one of the greenhouse gases and other atmospheric constituents, such as sulphate particles, chlorofluorocarbons (CFCs) and methane, also play a role. The effect of increased CO_2 is partly offset by natural and industrial pollution. One of the main pollutants is sulphate, which reflects some of the incoming radiation back to space. Scientists believe that the 20 million tonnes of sulphates emitted by the Mount Pinatubo volcano in the Philippines in 1991 was the cause of the cooling of the earth in the early 1990s. Furthermore, to make the predictions even more difficult, the expected rise in sea levels could be offset by increased snowfall in Antarctica (because of the effects of global warming on global weather patterns) and the subsequent growth of the ice cap.

The expected rise of sea level could have a pronounced effect on low lying areas such as deltas and coral reefs – 9% of Bangladesh and up to 15% of the Nile valley and delta could be inundated, reducing the amount of arable land considerably. Some eight million people in Egypt could be made homeless and many cities, including London, Los Angeles and Miami could be threatened.

heavy rain. Although storm surges present the major threat, coastal defences also may be overtopped or breached by wave action (caused by very violent storms and long distance waves) resulting in flood; recent examples in the UK are at Chiswell (Portland Island) (1979) and Towyn, Wales (1989) where this was the primary cause of flooding.

Major surges in the North Sea result from depressions tracking north-eastwards across northern Scotland. When the depression reaches the northern North Sea, the winds become northerly, helping the surge on its way northwards, whilst the Coriolis effect (the force generated by the earth's rotation) confines the surge to localised areas of the east coast of the UK. Such conditions were responsible for the east coast floods of January 1953 which affected areas from the Humber estuary to the Thames. Over 300 people were killed, over 800 square kilometres was flooded and the cost of the damage exceeded £50 million (Figure 6.8 on page 57). The conditions included:

- an intense low pressure system, 970 Mb, with winds of over 100 knots
- spring tides
- high river levels.

Figure 6.9 on page 57 shows the areas flooded. Following these floods, a national network of tide gauges and the Storm Tide Warning System (STWS) were established, to gather tidal information and to warn of any possible recurrences.

The Thames Barrier was completed in 1982 to protect London from the flooding which could result from a combination of surges and exceptionally high tides. The barrier has been erected at Greenwich on the tidal part of the Thames, and is designed to stop high tides and surges from affecting London. By lowering the barrage mechanism, high waters are prevented from travelling up the Thames. Levels of flooding in central London have been rising for a number of reasons:

- a rise in sea level
- the gradual subsidence in the south-east of England due to downwarping of the margins of the North Sea basin, due to isostatic readjustment. During the glacial period, Scotland was depresssed into the earth's crust by the sheer weight of ice on top of it. England, as a result, rose. As the glacier melted, the level of Scotland readjusted, and rose, with the consequence that the south of England fell, and continues to fall
- local subsidence which may be due to water abstraction and clay shrinkage.

The threat of flooding would be exacerbated by peak river flows. An early warning system which can predict exceptional levels from surge, tide and river flows several hours in advance gives time for the barrier to be closed.

Flooding in Bangladesh: storm surges and tropical cyclones

Another area where surges are a significant hazard is the delta of the River Ganges (Figure 6.10). Here surges may exceed four metres and the accompanying storm waves can add a further four metres to the water height; the funnel-shape of the Bay of Bengal forces water into a smaller surface area, and thus increases its height. Seven of the nine worst storms this century have affected Bangladesh. In 1970, over 300 000 people were killed in a surge. A further 225 000 people were killed in 1989 and in 1991 another 140 000 were killed in surges. In addition, millions were killed by the diseases and famines that followed, even more were made homeless and vast numbers of cattle were killed. Bangladesh is also subject to fierce tropical cyclones generally connected with the storm surges (see Chapter 8, Storms and hurricanes, for more on tropical cyclones).

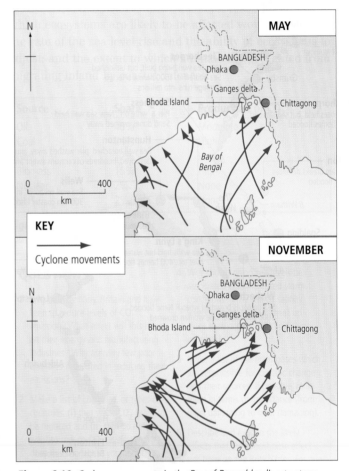

Figure 6.10 *Cyclone movements in the Bay of Bengal leading to storm surges in the Ganges Delta*
Source: Nagle, G. and Spencer, K., 1996, Investigating geography, Hodder and Stoughton

The risk of flooding in Bangladesh is increased because much of the country is a flat delta where the Ganges and Bramaphutra rivers drain into the Bay of Bengal, carrying 2 billion tonnes of fertile silt each year (Figure 6.11).

Bangladesh has a population of over 116 million on 144 000 square kilometres, giving it a density of over 800 people per square kilometre. The population pressure means that land must be farmed intensively; over two-thirds of Bangladesh is used for arable cultivation and of this 24% is irrigated. A large number of people have been attracted to the Ganges delta by its fertile silt and the availability of water – it is among the world's most densely populated areas. However, the people there are at risk from both river and coastal flooding.

Usually, the rivers flood annually in the monsoon period between June and September, covering up to 25% of the country and lining it with fertile silt. The river floods rarely cause deaths. It is the tropical cyclones in the Bay of Bengal that are largely responsible for the devastating floods which scourge Bangladesh.

On 29th April, 1991, the worst cyclone for nearly thirty years occurred. However, it was not unexpected. Its progress had been tracked from 25th April and scientists believed they had given ample warning. Winds of 145 mph created 4.5 metre waves and a storm surge which swept away whole communities. Some people were lucky – in the island of Sanadia, in the Ganges delta, 650 people climbed onto a 6 metre high cyclone shelter – and survived. Precautionary measures are expensive – it would cost over US$66 million to provide raised shelters for all of Bangladesh's 'at risk' population. So far, only 10% of the necessary shelters have been built. In addition, the country needs to repair the coastal embankments built in the 1960s which have been badly eroded over time.

There is concern about the impact of global warming upon Bangladesh (Figure 6.12). Rising sea levels, stronger storms and an increase in storm frequency, from global warming, could put more people at risk from coastal flooding.

Figure 6.11 Bangladesh's flat, low lying coastal areas

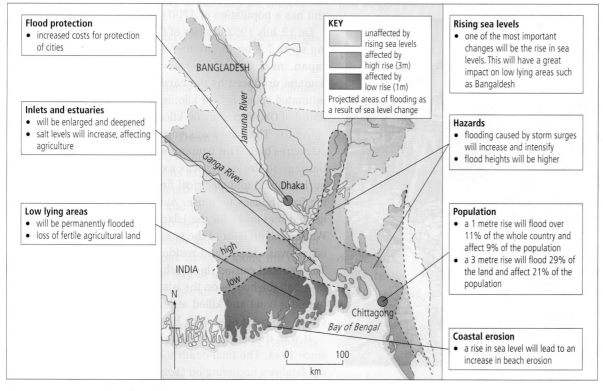

Figure 6.12 The possible effect of global warming on Bangladesh
Source: Nagle, G., 1998, Geography through diagrams, OUP

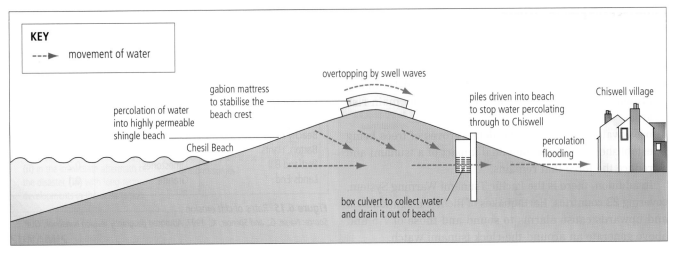

Figure 6.16 *Flood hazard at Chesil Beach*
Source: Nagle, G., 1998, Geography through diagrams, OUP

Portland was cut off from the mainland by flooding. The fishing community of Chiswell was devastated by the sea, in the worst sea flooding for over one hundred years. Within three months (February 1979), the sea swept into Chiswell once more, causing great damage to the hastily-restored buildings.

It is interesting to compare the characteristics of the two events. The December flood consisted of steep, erosive waves of about 12 second interval accompanied by a strong onshore wind. These waves, 4.5 metres high, on breaking on Chesil Beach, plunged at a steep angle creating a strong backwash which removed material from the beach in a seaward direction. As the storm continued, the beach was progressively cut back, which caused a lowering of the beach crest level. The beach crest level was further reduced by the overtopping water which also caused erosion of the landward face, assisted by the action of water percolating through the pebbles. These types of conditions bring the serious danger of a breach occurring if the storm were to last longer than that in December 1979 or if a second storm were to follow shortly after the first.

The February 1979 event was caused by an ocean swell with 18 second interval waves which arrived (unlike the 1978 storm) without warning and unaccompanied by strong winds. These swell waves, established far out at sea, produced much higher surge conditions and, although the deep-water wave-height was less than in 1978 and the waves were less steep, the increased run-up factor of these long-period waves led to much-increased overtopping of the beach and sea-wall, with tons of shingle being carried onto the landward side of the beach. When the seas subsided,

the beach was left in a very stable condition consisting of one long, continuous slope from the crest to the sea. This continuous slope, of course, assists overtopping to some extent and overtopping does progressively lower the crest, but it is most unlikely that a breach would occur under wave attack of this type.

To cope with the longstanding flooding problems, Weymouth Council specifies where new development can take place, and has requirements for special foundations and 'underflows' beneath properties to allow water to pass under the houses. Housing and other developments in Chiswell have openings or 'opes' between buildings to allow water to pass through, and houses which were once located at the back of the beach itself have been replaced by the sea wall and esplanade.

Since the late 1980s, over £4.5 million has been spent on a massive flood alleviation scheme for Chiswell. These sea defences safeguarded the community during the severe storms of January 1990. The sea defences which have been put in place as part of the flood alleviation scheme comprise metal cages called **gabions**, filled with pebbles from the beach, and an **intercepting drain** (box culvert) which takes water coming over and through the beach. The water is channelled away from residential properties and the road to Weymouth. A **gabion mattress** on the top of the beach limits the amount of material moved from and over the top of the beach. During recent storms, the flood alleviation scheme appears to have been successful in keeping flooding from overtopping to a minimum.

QUESTIONS

1 Explain why a sand and mud beach does not offer as much protection as a shingle beach.

2 Explain the high rates of coastal erosion in southern and eastern England.

3 Briefly describe the flood hazards at Chesil Beach. What measures have been taken to reduce the impact of flooding? How effective have they been?

Figure 6.17 *Flood defence measures at Chesil Beach*

SUMMARY

In this chapter we have seen that the range of hazards which affect coastal areas is wide. It is likely that the number of people who are at risk from such hazards will continue to increase because of the popularity of coasts as a place of residence. Many low-lying areas are densely populated and these areas are most at risk. We have seen how human activity can increase the risk of hazards, as well as providing structures to manage them. There is a wide difference between the impact of hazards in developed countries and developing countries.

QUESTIONS

1 With the use of examples, explain why some coastal areas are densely populated. What significance does this have in the management of natural hazards?
2 What is a storm surge? Under what conditions do storm surges occur? Compare the effect of the UK storm surge of 1953 with that in Bangladesh in 1991. Why did they differ?
3 With the use of examples, outline the risks posed by global warming.

BIBLIOGRAPHY AND RECOMMENDED READING

Blackmore, R. and Reddish, A., 1996, *Global environmental issues*, Hodder and Stoughton

Davies, J., 1980, *Geographical variations in coastline development*, Longman

Goudie, A. and Brunsden, D., 1994, *The environment of the British Isles*, Oxford

HMSO, 1992, *The UK Environment*, HMSO

Pethick, J., 1984, *An introduction to coastal geomorphology*, Arnold

Skinner, B. and Porter, S., 1995, *The dynamic earth*, Wiley

WEB SITES

Ministry of Agriculture, Fisheries and Food –
http://www.maff.gov.uk/
World wave heights –
http://www.oceanweather.com/data/data/htm

Chapter 7
Mountains, ice and their hazards

In this chapter we examine hazards associated with high altitudes (mountains and glaciers) and high latitudes (periglacial or tundra areas). In addition to a wide range of 'common' hazards, such as landslides, floods, and earthquakes, these areas are associated with avalanches and glacial surges. Mountains, glaciers and periglacial areas are very hazardous environments and increasing numbers of people are at risk, partly as a result of increasing tourism there. We begin this chapter with an overview of hazards in mountainous areas, and then look at the impact of skiing, avalanches, glacial surges and glacial bursts (jökulhlaups). Finally, we look at environmental hazards in periglacial areas, and look at the options for living in such areas. We finish by looking at the Alaska pipeline and oil spills in the Russian tundra.

MOUNTAIN ENVIRONMENTS

Mountainous areas commonly have high, rugged relief, steep slopes, and high rainfall. This combination makes them prone to high rates of run-off and erosion. Many mountainous areas are tectonic in origin (see Chapters 2 and 3) so are vulnerable to earthquakes and volcanic activity. Hazards which are largely limited to mountains include avalanches (Figure 7.1) and oxygen starvation (hypoxia). In many cases the potential for disasters is increasing due to human activities such as deforestation, the construction of large dams and the impact of tourism and recreation, especially skiing (Figure 7.2).

THE IMPACT OF SKIING ON MOUNTAIN AREAS

The environmental impacts of skiing are far reaching. They include the construction of ski pistes and related facilities such as access roads, parking, cafés and toilets. These have a major impact on the environment, such as an increase in levels of pollution, deforestation and soil erosion, and threaten delicate mountain ecosystems. Through deforestation, the infrastructure for skiing removes the natural protection against avalanches and degrades the natural landscape. New resort construction involves bulldozing, blasting, and reshaping of slopes. This increases slope instability and, together with deforestation, leads to a higher incidence of avalanches.

Western Europe is one of the most densely populated areas in the world, and mountains are one of the few remaining areas that are relatively uninhabited and untouched by human activity. However, mountain areas are

Figure 7.1 *Avalanche in mountainous environment*

Hazard	Disaster
Rockslides	Elm, Swiss Alps, 1881 Vaiont Dam, Italian Alps, 1963
Mud and debris flows	European Alps, 1987 Huanuco Province, Peru, 1989
Debris torrents	Coast Range, British Colombia Rio Colorado, Chile, 1987
Avalanches	Hakkari, Turkey, 1989 Western Iran, 1990
Earthquake-triggered mass movement	Campagna, Italy, 1980 Mount Ontake, Japan, 1984
Vulcanism-triggered mass movements	Mount St. Helens, USA, 1980 Nevado del Ruiz, Colombia, 1985
Weather-triggered mass movements from volcanoes	Mount Kelut, Indonesia, 1966 Mount Semeru, Java, 1981

Natural dams and dam-break floods:

- Landslide dams Indus Gorge, Western Himalayas, 1841; Ecuadorean Andes, 1987
- Glacier dams 'Ape Lake', British Colombia, 1984
- Moraine dams Khumbu, Nepal, Himalaya, 1985
- Avalanche dams Santa River, Peruvian Andes, 1962
- Vegetation dams New Guinea Highlands, 1970
- Artificial dam failures, Buffalo Creek, Appalachians, USA, 1972; Shanxi Province, China, 1989

Figure 7.2 *Examples of hazards in mountainous areas*
Source: based on Hewitt, K, 1997, Regions of risk, Longman

becoming increasingly popular destinations for tourists. Most tourism in the mountainous areas of Europe is concentrated in the Alps, which receives about 100 million tourists each year.

During the 1990s over fifty million people took an alpine ski holiday. By the late 1980s, over 40 000 ski runs and 14 000 ski lifts were needed to cope with the demand. The trend of development is well illustrated by the case of Switzerland where the number of installations has increased from about 250 in 1954 to nearly 2000 by 1990. Over 100 square kilometres of forest has been removed throughout the Alps and has led to higher rates of avalanches. In Austria, the creation of just 0.7 square kilometres of ski runs in 1980 for the Winter Olympics led to a major mud slide. As most visitors travel by car, exhaust fumes lead to further forest damage, as well as air pollution.

Another increasing hazard is water pollution and sewage disposal. In the French Pyrennes, sewage from summer tourist resorts discharges directly into streams. In the Alps, chemicals used in preparing 36 glaciers for skiing have caused increases in nitrogen and phosphorus levels in drinking water.

The unsustainable use of water is also increasing the potential for hazards. By 1992, 4000 snow cannons were producing artificial snow to lengthen the ski season in the Alps. These used 28 million litres of water per kilometre of piste. In Les Meunieres, France, 185 snow cannons installed for the 1992 Olympics were supplied from drinking water sources. The artificial snow used to extend the ski season melts slowly and reduces the already brief recuperation time for the alpine vegetation. Skiing in sparse snow conditions also contributes to erosion and damages sensitive vegetation. The result is a severe reduction in water absorption and holding capacity of mountain slopes. There is also an increased risk of run-off and avalanches.

When resorts experience low snow falls, skiers move higher up on to glaciers and higher lifts are used more regularly; summer skiing on the glaciers has extended the season. These trends increase the environmental problems because skiers are using a greater area, some of which is more sensitive.

At Jotunheimen in Norway, recreation has had a negative impact on animal species. Brown bears, wolverine, lynx, Arctic foxes, otters and even wild reindeer have all become less common. Road construction, power lines, visitor impact and long-range air pollution have all added to a decline in the wilderness value of the area and to the productivity of the ecosystem.

AVALANCHES

Avalanches are mass movements of snow and ice. An avalance may occur when newly-fallen snow slides off older snow, especially in winter, or in spring when partially-thawed snow moves, often triggered by skiing. Avalanches occur frequently on steep slopes over 22°, especially on north-facing slopes where the lack of sun inhibits the stabilisation of the snow. Average speeds in an avalanche are 40-60 kilometres per hour, but speeds of up to 200 kilometres per hour have been recorded in Japan.

Avalanches can be classified in a number of ways (Figure 7.3 on page 66). In the 1960s a distinction was made between airborne powder snow avalanches and ground-hugging avalanches. In 1979 a classification was made according to:

- the type of breakaway – from a point formed with loose snow, or from an area formed from a slab
- the position of the sliding surface – the whole snow cover or just the surface
- the form of the avalanche – whether in cross-section it is channelled or open
- the water content – dry or wet avalanches.

Although avalanches cannot be prevented, it is possible to reduce their impact (Figure 7.4 on page 66).

The underlying processes in an avalanche are similar to those in a landslide. In Chapter 4, Landslides and mass movements, we discussed in detail shear stress and shear strength. These factors are relevant here. Snow gets its strength from the interlocking of snow crystals and cohesion caused by electrostatic bonding of snow crystals. The snow remains in place as long as its strength is greater than the stress exerted by its weight and the slope angle.

The process is complicated by the way in which snow crystals constantly change. Changes in overlying pressure, compaction by freshly-fallen snow, temperature changes and the movement of meltwater through the snow, cause the crystal structure of the snow to change. It may become unstable and move downslope as an avalanche.

Loose avalanches, comprising fresh snow, usually occur soon after a snowfall. Slab avalanches occur after the snow has developed some cohesion. They are usually much larger than loose avalanches and cause more destruction. They are often started by a sudden rise in temperature which causes melting. The meltwater lubricates the slab, and makes it unstable. Many avalanches occur in spring (Figure 7.5, page 66) when the snowpack is large and temperatures are rising. Altitude and the number of avalanches are linked (Figure 7.6, page 66).

QUESTIONS

1 Describe and explain the effects of tourism on mountain areas. Use examples to support your answer.

2 How are pressures on mountain areas likely to change over the next few decades? Justify your answer.

(a)

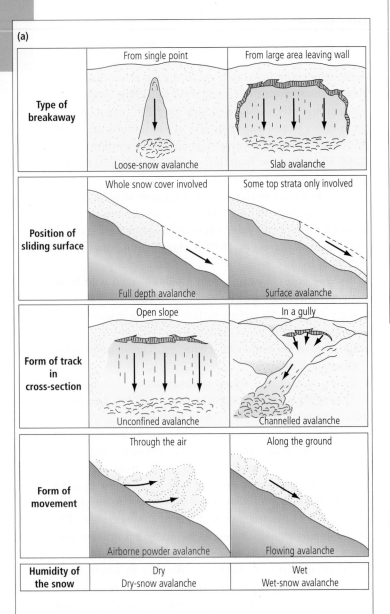

(b)

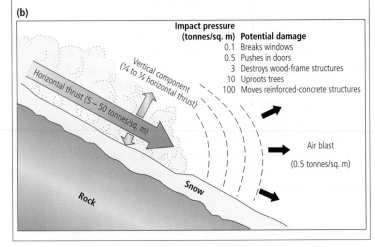

Figure 7.3 (a) *Avalanche classification,* **(b)** *Impact of a powder snow avalanche*
Source: Whittow, J., 1980, Disasters, Pelican

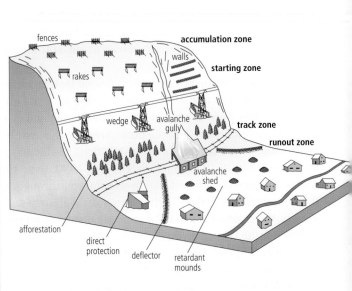

Figure 7.4 *Measures to reduce the impact of avalanches. The purpose of the structures in the accumulation and starting zones is snow retention; the purpose of the structures in the track and runout zones is avalanche deflection. Only one or two devices are likely to be in place in an avalanche-prone locality*
Source: Robinson, A., 1993, Earthshock, Thames and Hudson

December	10%
January	22%
February	32%
March	23%
April	13%

Figure 7.5
Occurrence of avalanches in the French Alps
Source: Data from Symons, L. and Morth, H., 1992, Avalanches, Geography review, 5, 4, 2–6

Altitude	No. of avalanches	Percent of total
3000 m and above	326	3
2500 – 2999 m	2210	24
2000 – 2499 m	3806	41
1500 – 1999 m	2632	28
Below 1500 m	394	4

Figure 7.6 *Avalanches and altitude in the Swiss Alps*
Source: Data from Symons, L. and Morth, H., 1992, Avalanches, Geography review, 5, 4, 2–6

QUESTIONS

1 Choose an appropriate method to display the data shown in Figure 7.5. Why are avalanches clustered in the months between January and March? Give at least **two** reasons.

2 Figure 7.6 shows how the distribution of avalanches in Switzerland varies with altitude. The tree-line is at about 1500 metres and the snow line is at about 3000 metres. Choose a suitable technique to show this distribution. How do you explain this pattern?

GLACIAL SURGES

Glacial surges are sudden wave-like motions travelling along a glacier in which velocities increase to between 10 and 100 times the normal rate. Typically, glaciers advance at speeds of between 4000 and 7000 metres per year (11 to 19 metres per day). Examples of surges include:

- Bruarjökull in Iceland, which moved 8 kilometres at speeds of up to 5 metres per hour
- the Variegated Glacier in Alaska, which moved at speeds of up to 65 metres per day in 1985
- the Hubbard Glacier in Alaska, which moved at up to 10 metres per day blocking off the Russell Fjord in August 1986, trapping dolphins and whales inside.

Why do glaciers surge? The velocity of a glacier is controlled by many factors. The most important include:

- the gradient of the rock floor
- the thickness of the ice, which controls pressure and melt-water
- the temperature within the ice.

During the 1980s and 1990s there has been considerable research into surges, although there is still uncertainty about:

- what mechanisms trigger the surge
- how and why are such high velocities achieved.

The cause of surges includes the sudden melting of ice, the very rapid accumulation of snow, avalanches, earthquakes (shock waves may 'shake' the glacier, and cause instability) and a build-up of subglacial meltwater under very high pressure.

Under normal conditions, the glacier has effective meltwater drainage through natural pipes and channels through and along it. However, with an increase in glacier thickness, subglacial channels are disrupted, leading to a decrease in permeability and a build-up of meltwater. The meltwater, which cannot escape, may 'lift' the glacier by up to a metre. These large volumes of meltwater increase the amount of basal sliding (movement of a glacier at its base). The glacier can withstand these pressures initially, but eventually is forced to surge.

The surge may alter the shape of the glacier. Increased slope angle may lead to more avalanches. The moving glacier may trigger avalanches as it carries snow and ice down the valley. The surge may also cause flooding as the ice thickens in winter and blocks off meltwater channels. It can erode considerable amounts of debris in the form of large boulders, which may threaten man-made structures, especially hydro-electric power stations and villages.

Figure 7.7 *Crevasse*

Within a moving glacier, different levels travel at different speeds. This causes crevasses to develop (Figure 7.7). In surging glaciers, these can be particularly hazardous as they can open and close in a matter of days.

JÖKULHLAUPS

A jökulhlaup is a flood caused by a glacier bursting. One of the largest jökulhlaups ever recorded took place in 1996; it was caused by tectonic activity beneath Europe's largest ice sheet, Iceland's Vatnajökull ice cap (Figure 7.8 on page 68).

On 19th September, 1996 an earthquake measuring 5.0 on the Richter scale was recorded from within Vatnajökull. This was followed by a swarm of smaller earthquakes which may have weakened the rock overlying the magma chamber of the volcano. On 2nd October the volcano erupted. The heat from the volcano caused large volumes of ice at the bottom of the icecap to melt. Within a couple of days the ice cap began to rise – by as much as 15 metres – and up to three cubic kilometres of water was dammed beneath the ice cap (Figure 7.9 on page 68).

QUESTIONS

1 What is a glacial surge?

2 Under what conditions do glacial surges occur?

3 Explain, with the use of examples, why glacial surges are environmental hazards.

Periglacial areas are fragile environments for two reasons:

1 The ecosystem is highly susceptible to interference because of the limited number and diversity of species involved. The extremely low temperatures limit decomposition, hence **pollution**, especially oil spills, has a very long lasting effect on periglacial ecosystems.

2 **Permafrost** is easily melted. Heat from buildings and pipelines and changes in the vegetation cover rapidly destroy permafrost (Figure 7.12). On bare ground, more heat is absorbed by the soil and is transmitted down. The higher temperatures melt the subsurface permafrost. Thawing of the permafrost increases the depth of the active layer and subsequent settlement of the soil causes subsidence.

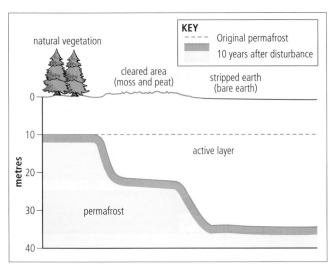

Figure 7.12 *The effect of removing vegetation in periglacial areas*
Source: Drew, D., 1984, Man-environment processes, Unwin Hyman

There has been a rapid increase in the human use of periglacial areas in recent decades. This is for reasons such as:

- mineral exploitation (such as oil in Alaska and Siberia, iron at Kiruna, Sweden)
- defence (for example, some countries maintaining their borders with the former USSR)
- tourism (Alps, Alaska)
- transport (trans-Alaska highway built for tourism and oil)
- social and economic change (Inuit in Canada – oil and tourism, former USSR).

The hazards associated with the use of periglacial areas are diverse and can be intensified by human impact. Problems include:

- mass movements such as avalanches
- solifluction (caused when flowing soil and water freeze in winter, then melt in the spring, carrying the soil downslope)
- rockfalls

- frost heave (frost heave can lift piles – foundations and pillars for buildings and roads – and other structures out of the ground)
- icing (a thin covering of ice over a road)
- flooding
- **thermokarst subsidence** (subsidence caused by seasonal changes in the permeabilty and volume of water/ice between summer and winter)
- low temperatures, a short growing season and a lack of light
- poor soils.

As we have seen, there are a number of ways in which people cope with hazards. They can:

- disregard them
- eliminate them
- design structures to withstand these stresses.

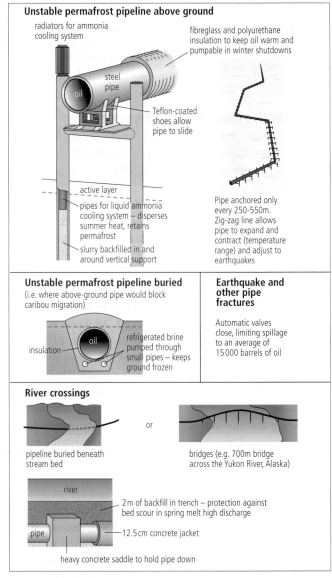

Figure 7.13 *Building strategies for pipelines in periglacial areas*
Source: Nagle, G. and Spencer, K., 1997, Advanced geography Revision Handbook, OUP

To overcome the problem of mass movement in the active layer, structures are built either on a thick bed of gravel or on stilts. For example, piles for carrying oil pipelines are embedded deep in the permafrost (Figure 7.13) – in Prudhoe Bay, Alaska, the piles are 11 metres deep. This method of construction is extremely expensive: each pile cost over US$3000, in the early 1970s, US$18 000 in today's terms.

Services are difficult to provide in periglacial environments. It is impossible to lay underground networks. Hence **utilidors** (insulated water and sewage pipes) are provided above ground. Waste disposal is also difficult owing to the low temperatures.

ENVIRONMENTAL CONCERNS IN ALASKA

The Alaska pipeline carries oil from Prudhoe in the north of Alaska to Anchorage in the south. The engineering implications and the environmental effects of the scheme were, and are, far reaching.

1   Disturbance was caused to the vegetation and soil in transporting and installing the pipeline: these could have been reduced if work had been done in the winter.
2   Scarring by tractors created tramlines for overland water flow and the development of thermokarst.
3   In the initial construction, large quantities of gravel from the river were used to insulate the permafrost. This had the effect of increasing the rate of erosion, and affected stream flows, sediment transport and fish spawning grounds and created flooding.
4   Once completed, the pipeline suffered from breakages and oil spills, and thawing and erosion along the pipeline from the heat of the pipe, and the weight (pressure). If oil is spilled, the permafrost does not allow downward percolation, so the oil saturates the active layer and destroys the local ecosystem.

5   The problem of oil spillage on land or at sea is greatly magnified in cold environments, as it takes longer for the waste matter to break down.
6   The behavioural reaction of animals (migration, feeding, reproduction, feeding) to the pipeline and the terminals is unknown but likely to be negative.
7   Increased facilities along the maintenance roads to provide services for travellers further disrupt the migratory paths of caribou.
8   Conflict between humans and wildlife, notably bears and wolves, occurs in the vicinity of rubbish dumps.
9   There is an ever-present threat of earthquakes along the natural tectonic boundaries
10 Oil is spilled offshore as ballast disposal from tankers – the detrimental effect on fishing in the Prince William Sound is estimated at US$10 m each year.

THE RUSSIAN TUNDRA: SCENE OF EUROPE'S BIGGEST OIL SPILL

According to the US Department of Energy, the oil spill at Usinsk in northern Russia in October 1994 was the third largest in history (Figure 7.14). It caused an oil slick 11 kilometres long, 12 metres wide and a metre deep. Experts' concerns are focused on three issues:

- the cash-starved, recently-privatised oil producers who control thousands of kilometres of pipeline show little regard for environmental issues
- engineering problems are intensified by the presence of permafrost: the combination of the weight of the pipeline and the heat it gives off causes the permafrost to melt, land to subside and pipes to fracture
- decomposition of oil is extremely slow in cold climates as bacterial activity is greatly reduced.

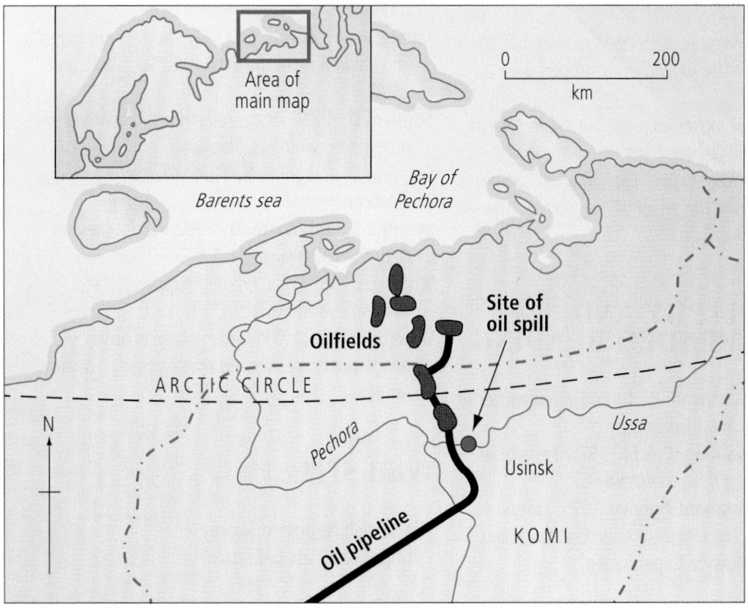

Figure 7.14 *The Russian oil spill, October 1994*
Source: Nagle, G. and Spencer, K., 1996, Investigating geography, Hodder and Stoughton

According to Komi herdsmen in northern Russia close to the oil spill at Usinsk, reindeer are suffering from blindness and birth defects. Environmentalists claim that sulphur dioxide is released when the oil spills and that this and other trace elements affect the metabolism of the reindeer. The Russian environmental ministry now admits that between 90 000 and 120 000 tonnes of oil were spilled in the Usinsk disaster: this is about twice the size of the Exxon Valdez disaster in Alaska in 1989. The costs of attempts to clean up the oil spill proved to be prohibitive. The scale of the disaster was not seen until the snow melted in the spring, bringing the oil into Russia's rivers and seas.

However, this may be only the tip of the iceberg: the Russian authorities are now saying that as much as 70% of pipelines are potentially dangerous, because of leaking oil. Leaks have occurred in Russia over a number of years but have been increasing in frequency since 1993; experts are worried that millions of barrels of oil leak every year from Russian pipelines.

Similarly, the Nyenski tribe in the Yamal Peninsula of Siberia have suffered as a result of the exploitation of oil and gas. Oil leaks, subsidence of railway lines, destruction of vegetation, decreased fish stocks, pollution of breeding grounds and reduced caribou numbers have all happened directly or indirectly as a result of man's attempt to exploit this remote and inhospitable environment.

Figure 7.15 *The aftermath of the Siberian oil spill in October 1994*

QUESTIONS

1 What are the problems in trying to develop periglacial areas? In what ways have levels of development affected the use of periglacial environments?

2 Explain why oil pollution is a particular problem in periglacial areas.

3 Suggest contrasting reasons why hazards in periglacial regions are increasing.

SUMMARY

Mountains and glaciers have a rugged appeal. They may appear tranquil but, as we have seen in this chapter, they are severe environments. In fact, they form some of the most hazardous places on earth. This is partly due to variable temperatures, steep gradients, high altitude and, in the case of mountains, their tectonic origin. We have also seen that periglacial environments are hazardous environments. These fragile environments are facing increasing pressures from people and it looks as though environmental hazards are likely to increase there as more people use them, for whatever reason.

QUESTIONS

1 What are the hazards associated with mountain environments? Use examples to support your answer.

2 With the use of examples, examine the impact of skiing upon the environment.

3 Why do avalanches occur? Explain what can be done to minimise the effect of avalanches. (Use Figure 7.4 to help you.)

BIBLIOGRAPHY AND RECOMMENDED READING

Briggs, D. and Smithson, P., 1985, *Fundamentals of physical geography*, Hutchinson

Embleton, C. and King, C.A.M., 1975, *Periglacial geomorphology*, Edward Arnold

European Environment Agency, 1995, *Europe's Environment: The Dobris Assessment*, European Environment Agency, Copenhagen

French, H.M., 1976, *The periglacial environment*, Longman

Jenner, P. and Smith, C., 1992, *The Tourism Industry and Environment*, The Economist Special Report, 2453

Sugden, D., 1982, *Arctic and Antarctic: a modern geographic synthesis*, Blackwell

Sugden, D. and John, B., 1976, *Glaciers and landscape*, Arnold

Symons, L. and Morth, H., 1992, *Avalanches, Geography Review*, 5, 4, 2-6

Warren, C., 1995, *Ice, fire and flood in Iceland*, Geography Review, 10, 4, 2-6

Washburn, A.L., 1979, *Geocryology: a survey of periglacial processes and environments*, Edward Arnold

WEB SITE

The British Antarctic Survey – http://www.nerc-bas.ac.uk/

Chapter 8
Storms and hurricanes

Over the next three chapters we consider atmospheric hazards such as storms and hurricanes, drought and air quality. There is a considerable human element in turning a hazard into a disaster. In this chapter we concentrate upon storms and hurricanes (Figure 8.1). These are terms that are often confused. We start, therefore, with a classification of storms and look at a model of a simple low pressure system. Then we examine the nature and effects of hazards related to storms, gales, hurricanes and tornadoes. As we have seen in Chapter 6, Coastal hazards, atmospheric hazards such as tropical cyclones interact with other hazards to create features such as storm surges, flooding and landslides.

LOW PRESSURE SYSTEMS

In mid-latitude areas (between 40° and 60°), such as the UK, the weather is dominated by low pressure systems. These are formed by the mixing of warm tropical air and cold polar air. When these two bodies of air meet, the lighter, warm air rises over the denser, cold air to form a low pressure system (also termed a depression or a cyclone).

Figure 8.2 shows a very simplified model of a low pressure system. (Just as we would not expect any city to fit exactly Burgess's model of land-use, we should not expect any weather system to match this model exactly. But we

Figure 8.1 Tornado

would expect them to resemble the model in parts.) The cold air pushes the warm air off the ground. As the warm air rises it cools, condenses and forms clouds from which rain falls. The cause of the uplift is the difference in density

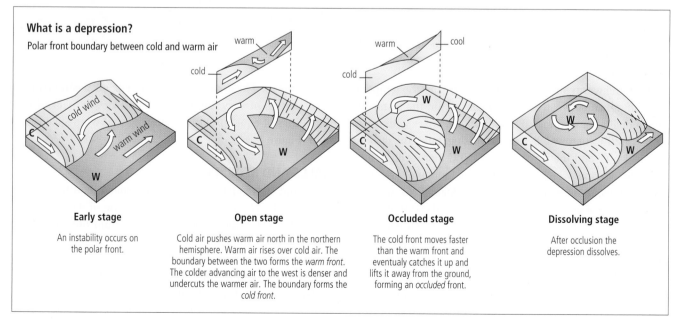

What is a depression?
Polar front boundary between cold and warm air

Early stage	Open stage	Occluded stage	Dissolving stage
An instability occurs on the polar front.	Cold air pushes warm air north in the northern hemisphere. Warm air rises over cold air. The boundary between the two forms the *warm front*. The colder advancing air to the west is denser and undercuts the warmer air. The boundary forms the *cold front*.	The cold front moves faster than the warm front and eventually catches it up and lifts it away from the ground, forming an *occluded* front.	After occlusion the depression dissolves.

Figure 8.2 Life-cycle of a typical mid-latitude depression
Source: Nagle, G. and Spencer, K., 1997, Advanced geography, OUP

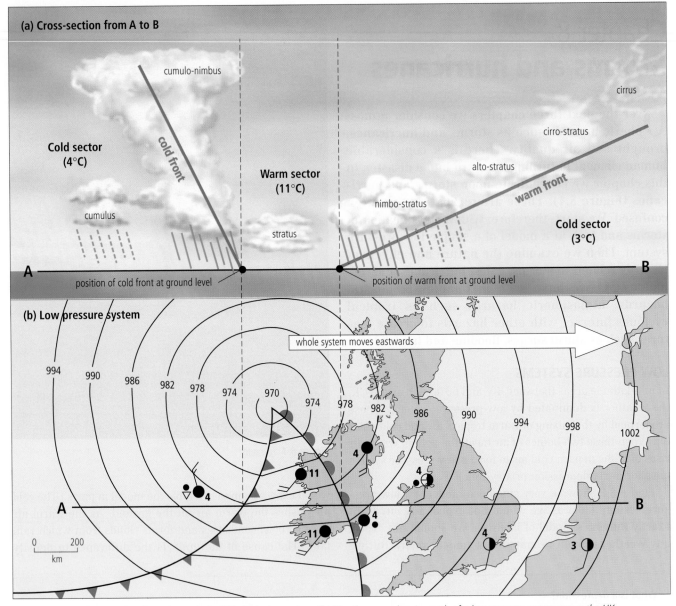

(a) Cross-section from A to B

cumulo-nimbus

cirrus

cirro-stratus

alto-stratus

Cold sector
(4°C)

cold front

Warm sector
(11°C)

warm front

nimbo-stratus

Cold sector
(3°C)

cumulus

stratus

A

B

position of cold front at ground level

position of warm front at ground level

(b) Low pressure system

whole system moves eastwards

994 990 986 982 978 974 970 974 978 982 986 990 994 998 1002

A

B

0   200
km

Figure 8.3 (a) Cross-section through a typical mid-latitude depression, (b) Weather map showing path of a low pressure system across the UK
Source: Nagle, G. and Spencer, K., 1997, Skills and techniques in geography, Stanley Thornes

between the warm and the cold air. The greater the temperature difference between the two bodies of air, the faster the rate of uplift. For example, if cold air of 3°C mixes with warm air of 18-20°C there will be vigorous rising, but if the cold air is only 4-6°C, and the warm air is 8-10°C there will be little uplift. Jet streams which are found near the top of low pressure systems, at an altitude of about 10 kilometres, will also affect the rate of uplift. These very strong winds (100-300 kilometres per hour) help to draw air up a low pressure system.

Most of the rain, strong winds and pressure changes are found at weather fronts, where the cold air and the warmer air meet. In a typical low pressure system there are distinct weather changes at the fronts (Figure 8.3 a). In winter, when there is a greater contrast between the temperature of tropical air and polar air, depressions are stronger and have

more energy. These depressions appear on weather maps with centres of very low pressure and closely packed isobars (lines of equal pressure) showing that wind speeds are high (Figure 8.3 b).

GALES AND STORMS

Gales and storms have a lower wind speed than hurricanes (Figure 8.4). The Beaufort Scale is a scale of wind velocity, with 12 levels. Wind velocity is not constant but consists of stronger gusts and calmer lulls, so the levels in the Beaufort Scale correspond to a range of wind speeds.

Gales and storms (and hurricanes) are a natural process by which the atmosphere attempts to even out temperature differences around the world. There is an excess of heat in equatorial areas and an excess of cold in polar areas. Winds and ocean currents transfer stores of heat from the tropics towards the poles and carry some of the cold air and water from the poles towards the tropics. Between 40° and 60° (the mid-latitudes) these two contrasting flows meet.

Force	Description	Commonly observed effects on land	Speed (km/hr)
0	Calm	Smoke rises vertically	less than 1
1	Light air	Direction of wind shown by smoke drift but not wind vanes	1-5
2	Light breeze	Wind felt on face; leaves rustle; ordinary vane moved by wind	6-11
3	Gentle breeze	Leaves and small twigs in gentle motion; wind extends light flag	12-19
4	Moderate breeze	Raises dust and loose paper; small branches are moved	20-29
5	Fresh breeze	Small trees in leaf begin to sway, small branches are moved	30-39
6	Strong breeze	Large branches in motion; whistling heard in telephone wires; umbrellas used with difficulty	40-50
7	Moderate gale	Whole trees in motion; inconvenience felt when walking against wind	51-61
8	Fresh gale	Twigs break off trees; progress generally impeded	62-74
9	Strong gale	Slight structural damage occurs (chimney pots and slates removed)	75-87
10	Whole gale	Seldom experienced inland; trees uprooted; considerable structural damage occurs	88-101
11	Storm	Very rarely experienced; accompanied by widespread damage	102-120
12	Hurricane	Extremely rare; serious damage; visibility at sea extremely poor	Above 120

Figure 8.4 The Beaufort Scale of wind force

Severe gales and storms in the UK

In the UK, gales and storms are more likely to develop in the winter months, when the difference in temperature between the weather systems is greater. The mid-latitude depressions from which they develop become deep weather systems (areas of very low pressure, for example 970 – 980 Mb) of great power and force.

The Great Gale of October 1987 was one of the most severe storms ever to hit the south of Britain (Figure 8.5). It

started as a low pressure system off the coast of Spain and was dragged north-eastwards to the UK by high-level jet streams. Some of its energy was supplied by warm waters from the Bay of Biscay, evaporating into the atmosphere. The low pressure was caused by temperture differences between the air masses, and also vigorous jet stream (upper wind) activity sucking up air from ground level, thereby initiating and intensifying the centre of low pressure.

This was the strongest gale to affect much of the UK for up to 250 years, bringing with it gusts of up to 166 kilometres per hour (104 miles per hour). The worst gusts were during the night – had they been during the daytime the

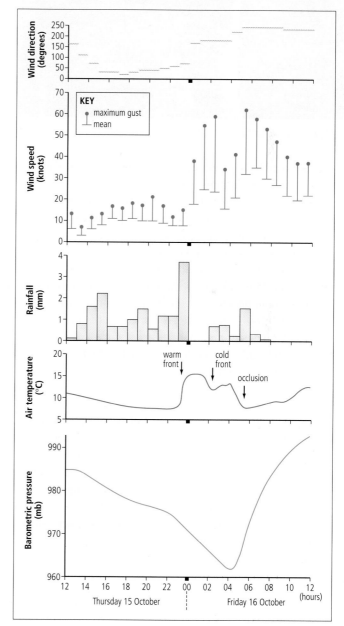

Figure 8.5 Weather data collected in Oxford between midday, 15th October and midday, 16th October, 1987
Source: Coones, P., 1987, The Great Gale of 16 October, 1987, Geography review, 1, 3, 6-10

QUESTION

1 What is the difference between the following pairs: storms and hurricanes; moderate breeze and fresh breeze; fresh gale and strong gale?

Figure 8.6 *Damage caused by the Great Gale of 1987*

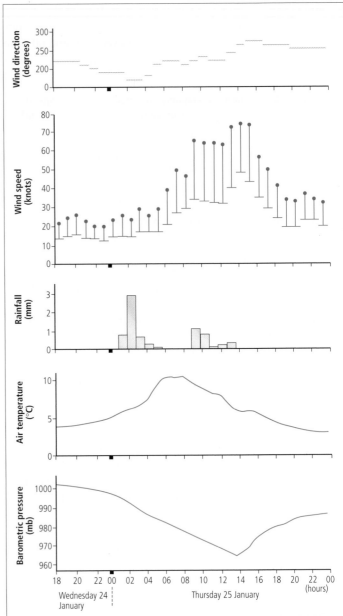

Figure 8.7 *Weather data collected at Oxford during the passage of the depression which caused the storm of January 1990*
Source: Burt, T. and Coones, P., 1990, The winds of change, Geography review, 3, 5, 22-8

effects would have been much greater (Figure 8.6). The total costs of insurance claims were over £860 million.

Although the 1987 gale had a recurrence interval of 250 years (meaning that, on average, we would not expect a storm of similar intensity for another 250 years), there was another severe storm in January 1990. This storm was called a 'bomb', a term used to describe low pressure systems which intensify by 24 millibars (mb) in 24 hours. (A 'normal' fall in pressure, at the beginning of a more regular storm, might be 10 mb. The greater the fall, and the speed of the fall, the faster and more destructive the wind speeds.) Like the 1987 gale, it was closely related to the location of jet stream activity. One theory is that jet stream activity intensified during the 1980s as a result of global warming and a series of warm summers in the UK.

The 1990 storm developed over the Atlantic and was easier to detect and predict than the 1987 storm, because the 1990 storm travelled due west; the 1987 storm travelled up, by surprise, from the Bay of Biscay. It affected a much larger part of the UK, with gusts of up to 118 kph (74 mph) (Figure 8.7). (8 kmph equals 5 knots.) Like the 1987 gale, it was a low frequency, high magnitude event, but its effects on the UK were different (Figure 8.8).

The comparison of these two similar natural events shows several elements that affect the nature of a disaster. These include:

- the time of day
- areal extent of the storm
- the time of year
- awareness of the event
- precautions taken
- the duration of the event
- the strength of the storm or hazard.

	16 October 1987	25 January 1990
Meteorological parameters		
Fall in pressure	30 mb in 30 hours	39 mb in 24 hours
Maximum gust	100 knots	93 knots
Return period of an event of this magnitude	Greater than 200 years	150 years
Area of Britain mainly affected		
Onshore	South-east England	Most of southern Britain, especially the south west
Offshore	English Channel and North Sea	Most sea areas around Britain
Timing	Middle of night	Daytime
Season	Autumn	Winter
Effects		
Human fatalities	19	47
Trees blown down	15 000 000	5 000 000
Insurance claims	£1 117 000 000	Considerably more
Other effects	Worst power failure in south-east England since WWII, 3000 miles of telephone lines brought down	Several hundred thousand homes without power
Summary	'The worst, most widespread night of disaster in the south east of England since 1945' (Home Secretary, Douglas Hurd). The timing meant that weekend was available for restoration of services, thereby limiting the disruption of commerce, industry and schooling	Greater damage and death toll than 1987 on account of: • wider area affected • daytime occurrence • significance of successive, sustained gusts of high strength • progressive weakening of buildings and structures • restoration hampered by bad weather

Figure 8.8 A comparison of the storms of 1987 and 1990
Source: Burt, T., and Coones, P., 1990, The winds of change, Geography review, 3, 5, 22-8

QUESTIONS

1 Study Figure 8.5 which shows the weather at Oxford during the passage of the Great Gale.

(a) Describe how wind speeds and wind gusts varied with the passage of the storm.

(b) Describe the changes in weather as **(i)** the warm front and **(ii)** the cold front pass over.

(c) Briefly give **two** reasons why the Great Gale caused so much damage in southern England.

2 With reference to the storms of 1987 and 1990, explain briefly how any **three** of the following affect the outcome of an environmental hazard: the time of day; areal extent; the time of year; awareness of the event; precautions taken.

TROPICAL STORMS: HURRICANES

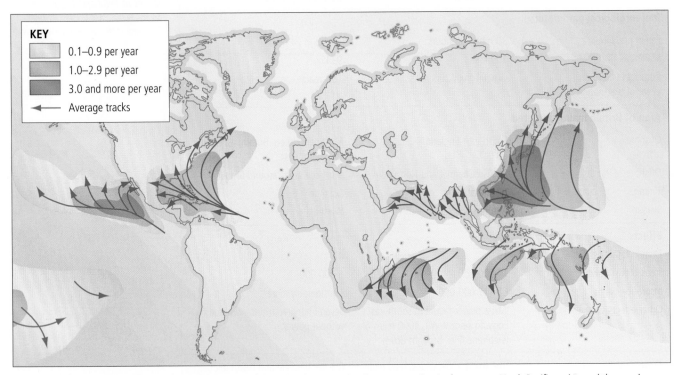

Figure 8.9 *The location and average annual frequency of tropical cyclones. Notice the concentration in the western North Pacific region and the way in which the storm tracks curve polewards threatening populated coastal areas*
Source: Smith, K., 1992, Environmental hazards, Routledge

Hurricanes, typhoons and tropical cyclones are among the most violent storms that affect the world. Figure 8.9 shows that they affect a very large area. The amount of energy produced in a single hurricane would be enough to supply the whole of the USA with all its electricity for six months.

Hurricanes are compound hazards which include heavy rainfall, strong winds and high waves which can cause other hazards such as flooding and mudslides. They are intense

Figure 8.10 *Structure of a hurricane showing **(a)** a plan view with wind directions and main cloud features, **(b)** vertical cross-section*
Source: Musk, L. F., 1988, Weather systems, CUP

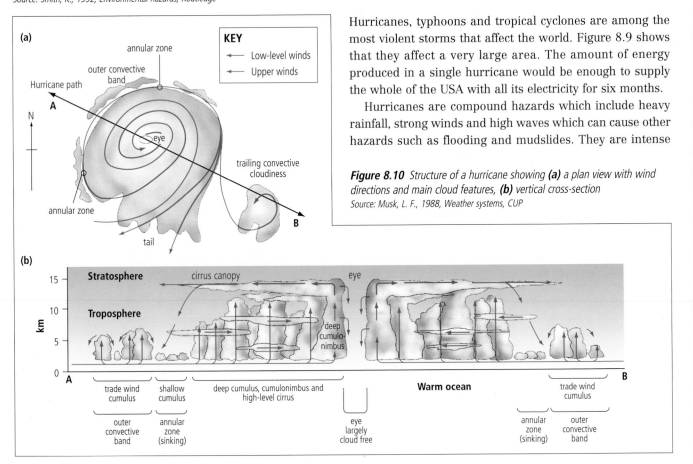

hazards which affect a large area but are difficult to predict accurately. The onset of any individual hurricane is rapid. They may travel slowly at first but their path is erratic. Hence it is not always possible to give more than twelve hours notice – the generally accepted minimum time for evacuation and precautionary procedures to be effective.

Hurricanes develop as intense low pressure systems over tropical oceans. Winds spiral rapidly around a calm central area known as the eye (Figure 8.10). The diameter of the whole hurricane may be as much as 800 kilometres, although the very strong winds which cause most of the damage are found in a narrower belt up to 300 kilometres wide. The 'Great Gale' that brought chaos to southern England in 1987, was not by definition a hurricane as it did not originate over a tropical ocean, although its wind speed was hurricane force on the Beaufort Scale. It was called a hurricane in much of the media.

Figure 8.11 *Satellite picture of Fran, hurricane 4 September 1996*

Hurricanes move excess heat from low latitudes to higher latitudes (Figure 8.11). They normally develop in the westward-flowing air just north of the equator (known as an easterly wave). They begin life as small-scale tropical disturbances or tropical depressions which cause warm air to rise. Tropical disturbances create thunder storms which persist for at least twenty-four hours. These may develop into tropical storms, which have wind speeds of up to 117 kmph (73 mph). However, only about 10% of tropical disturbances ever become hurricanes, that is, storms with wind speeds above 118 kmph (above 74 mph).

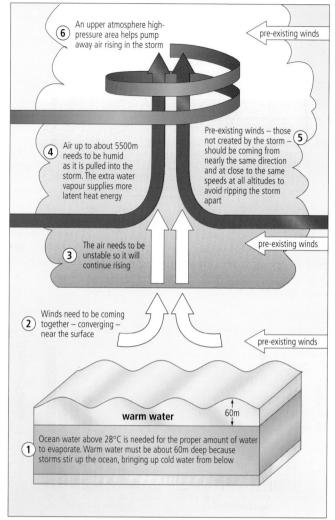

Figure 8.12 *Factors required for the development of a hurricane*
Source: Slattery, M. and Burt, T., 1997, Geography review 10, 3, 12–7

For hurricanes to form, a number of conditions are needed (Figure 8.12):
- sea temperatures must be over 27°C (warm water gives off large quantities of heat when it is condensed – this is the heat which drives the hurricane)
- the low pressure area has to be sufficiently far from the equator so that the Coriolis force (the force caused by the rotation of the earth) creates rotation in the rising air mass – if the low pressure area is close to the equator there is insufficient rotation and a hurricane cannot develop.

Once the rising air has become established in the form of a convection cell, the system is self-perpetuating as long as conditions remain favourable. The rising air releases large quantities of heat during condensation. This reinforces the instability (rising of air) within the hurricane. At the eye, air descends from the top of the system. As it does so, it is warmed and is therefore able to hold more moisture. Hence condensation is reduced and the eye remains cloudless.

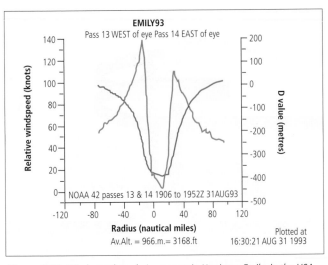

Figure 8.13 *Wind speeds and air pressure in Hurricane Emily, in the USA, August, 1993*
Source: Slattery, M. and Burt, T., 1997, Geography review 10, 3, 12-7

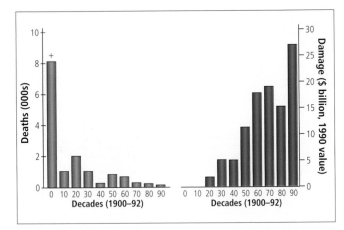

Figure 8.14 *Deaths and damage caused by hurricanes in the USA, 1900-92*
Source: National Hurricane Center, USA

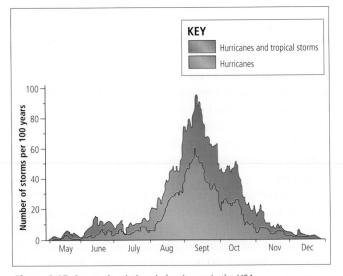

Figure 8.15 *Seasonal variations in hurricanes in the USA*
Source: Neumann, C. J., Jarvinen, B. R. and Pike, A. C., 1990, Tropical cyclones of the North Atlantic Ocean, National Climatic Date Center, Asheville, North Carolina

In a mature hurricane, pressure may fall to as low as 880-970 millibars. This, and the strong contrast in pressure between the eye and outer part of the hurricane, leads to gale force winds (Figure 8.13). A mature hurricane is typically 200-500 kilometres in diameter, with clouds up to 12 kilometres in height.

Hurricanes are also characterised by enormous quantities of water, due to their origin over moist tropical seas. Intense rainfall, up to 500 millimetres in 24 hours, invariably causes flooding. Hurricane winds can cause 15 metre waves in the open ocean. Peak heights of these waves on the land can be as high as 6 metres.

Hurricanes create a major threat to human life, property and economic activities (Figure 8.14). They are a seasonal hazard (Figure 8.15), peaking between June and November in the Northern Hemisphere and December to April in the Southern Hemisphere. Because of their impact, and the cost of the destruction they cause, they are monitored intensely by satellite, and hurricane paths are predicted by complex computer programmes.

The hurricane hazard is greatest on islands and coastal areas. Once a hurricane starts to move inland, it is deprived of its source of heat and moisture and begins to decay. Nevertheless, many hurricanes persist over land for hundreds of kilometres, as intense frontal depressions (low pressure systems), and cause serious damage, albeit not on the same scale as when they were hurricanes on the coast.

Hurricanes in the USA

Three of the most destructive hurricanes in recent years in the USA have been Hurricane Gilbert (1988), Hurricane Hugo (1989) and Hurricane Andrew (1992). Gilbert led to the loss of 315 lives and estimated costs of over US$5 billion; Hugo was responsible for only 49 deaths but cost an estimated US$10 billion; Andrew caused 62 deaths and cost between US$20 billion and US$30 billion damage.

The number of people in the USA living in 'at risk areas' is increasing as people choose to live in coastal areas which are affected by hurricanes, such as Florida: the proportion of people living within 50 kilometres of the coast is set to rise from 50% in 1990 to 75% by 2010. In 1992, a US survey suggested that between 80% and 90% of the population had never experienced a Category 3 hurricane (Figure 8.16). This created a false sense of security and the population tends to underestimate the risk of hurricane damage. The damage caused by Hurricane Andrew in Southern Florida, Louisiana, and then Mississippi, was increased by the general trend of people moving into hurricane affected areas. Hurricane Andrew produced sustained winds of 230 kmph (145 mph) and gusts of over 280 kmph (175 mph), destroying 60 000 homes. It was a Category 5 hurricane (Insets 8.2 and 8.3).

Inset 8.1
Hurricane Hugo, September 1989

Hurricanes and tropical storms are named alphabetically, hence Hugo was the eighth
hurricane in the world in 1989. It was the worst storm for over ten years and wind speeds of
over 240 kmph (150 mph) were recorded. Hugo caused terrible damage on many islands in
the Caribbean and on the eastern coast of the USA. In some coastal towns in Guadeloupe
over 90% of the buildings were seriously damaged. Montserrat, the Virgin Islands, Dominica,
Antigua and Puerto Rica were seriously affected by flooding and landslides. Although the
hurricane reached the USA at Charleston in South Carolina, warnings had been issued and
precautions taken to minimise the risk. Thousands were made homeless but the loss of life
was kept down.

Inset 8.2
The Saffir Simpson scale

Type	Category	Damage	Pressure (mb)	Windspeed (mph)	Storm surge (ft)
Depression	–	–	–	>35	–
Tropical storm	–	–	–	36 – 73	–
Hurricane	1	Minimal	>980	74 – 95	4–5
Hurricane	2	Moderate	965 – 979	96 – 110	6–8
Hurricane	3	Extensive	945 – 964	111 – 130	9–12
Hurricane	4	Extreme	920 – 944	131 – 155	13–18
Hurricane	5	Catastrophic	<920	>155	>18

Figure 8.16
The Saffir-Simpson scale

The Saffir-Simpson scale was developed by the National
Oceanic and Atmospheric Administration and assigns
hurricanes to one of five categories of potential disaster.

Category 1 Winds 74-95 mph (118-152 kmph) will cause no
real damage to solid building structures. Damage to mobile
homes and vegetation is likely, some minor coastal road
flooding and pier damage is predicted.

Category 2 Winds 96-110 mph (154-176 kmph) will cause
some damage to roofing material, doors and windows of
buildings. Considerable damage to vegetation, piers and
mobile homes is expected. Flooding of coastal and low-lying
escape routes can be expected 2-4 hours before the arrival of
the storm centre.

Category 3 Winds 111-130 mph (178-208 kmph) are likely to
cause damage to small residences and utility buildings with a
minor number of curtain-wall failures. Flooding near the coast
will destroy smaller structures whilst larger structures may be
damaged by floating debris. Land continuously less than
1.5 metres (about 5 feet) above sea level may be flooded
up to 8 kilometres (5 miles) inland.

Category 4 Winds 131-155 mph (210-248 kmph) are likely
to result in more extensive curtain-wall failures, with some
complete roof destruction on smaller properties.
Structures near the shore may be subject to severe lower
floor damage, and the evacuation of all residential areas
less than 3 metres (10 feet) above sea level for up to
10 kilometres (6 miles) inland is likely to be necessary. Major
erosion of beach areas is also expected.

Category 5 Winds greater than 155 mph (248 kmph) are
likely to result in complete roof failure on many residential
and industrial buildings. Major damage to lower floors of all
structures less than 3 metres (10 feet) above sea level, and
some complete building failures are likely. Evacuation of all
residential areas on low ground within 16-24 kilometres
(10-15 miles) of the shoreline is expected to be necessary.

Governments are faced with difficult decisions when a hurricane is predicted – localised conditions make it almost impossible to predict where the hurricane will make the most impact and, in addition, it is very costly to evacuate an area. It is estimated that the cost of evacuating a 500 kilometre stretch of the US coastline is about US$50 million, due to losses in business, tourism, protection measures and so on.

Hurricane activity in 1995

Hurricane activity increased in 1995. Up to eleven hurricanes and eight tropical storms were responsible for 121 deaths and US$7.7 billion of damage. The reason for the increase in hurricane activity in 1995 is complex and can be related to five interacting factors:

1 El Nino – the cold water current off the coast of Peru was replaced in 1995 by a warm current, El Nino. This generated winds which flowed in a westerly direction from the eastern Pacific across to the Atlantic Ocean. El Nino ended in 1995 and normal wind directions returned.

2 Rainfall in West Africa – high rainfall in West Africa is related (although the relationship is not understood) to the formation of storms off the African coast and hurricanes in the USA.

3 Temperatures and pressure in West Africa – when surface water temperatures are higher and air pressure is lower than normal in West African coastal regions, southerly winds are formed; these help to turn tropical disturbances into hurricanes.

4 Stratospheric winds – when these blow from the west there is more hurricane activity. Stratospheric winds often reverse after about a year.

5 Tropospheric winds – winds at 10-12 km above sea level are heavily influenced by El Nino, rainfall in Africa and sea pressure in the Caribbean. Stronger tropospheric (west) winds reduce hurricane activity by blowing the hurricanes out to sea.

Inset 8.3
The El Nino effect

The unusual weather events of 1997, such as the flooding in central Europe and the drought in Korea and China, have been linked to an early and forceful appearance of the El Nino weather system. El Nino, which means the Christ Child, is an irregular occurrence of a current of warm surface water in the Pacific Ocean off the coast of South America. In the 1980s it was said to be a nine-year occurrence – in the 1990s this was shown to be wrong. El Nino causes large-scale changes in ocean temperatures and ocean currents which disrupt the world's wind and rainfall patterns. In July 1997, the sea surface temperature in the eastern tropical Pacific was 2.0-2.5°C above normal, breaking all previous records. The El Nino's peak temperature continued into early 1998, after which weather conditions returned to normal.

The El Nino event that started in the summer of 1997 could be even more catastrophic than the 1982-3 El Nino which claimed nearly 2000 lives and caused over US$13 billion damage to property and crops. Among the short-term effects, for 1998, of the 1997-98 El Nino, scientists have predicted:

- a stormy winter in California (the 1982-83 event took 160 lives and caused US$2 billion damage in floods and mudslides)
- above average rainfall in the south of the USA
- increased rates of erosion
- worsening drought in Australia, Indonesia, the Philippines, southern Africa and north-east Brazil
- increased risk of malaria in South America
- lower rainfall in northern Europe
- higher rainfall in southern Europe.

For example, in 1997 the tropical island of Papua New Guinea (PNG) experienced an unprecedented six-month drought which lead to the death of hundreds of indigenous people. In the western half of the island over 400 people have died from malnutrition. The usual cycles of heavy tropical rain have been delayed and the drought has been intense. Mountain streams and 10-metre deep wells have dried up. Severe frosts – the worst in living memory – added to the problems caused by the drought. Of the 3.5 million people, 85% are subsistence farmers, many depending on the sweet potato. Drought and frosts have destroyed the crop and farmers have been forced to forage from the forest in order to survive. In the worst hit areas people are surviving on leaves collected from the rain forest.

QUESTIONS

1 Describe and account for the relationship between air pressure and wind speed in a hurricane, as shown in Figure 8.13.

2 Study Figure 8.14 which shows the relationship between the number of deaths and the cost of damage caused by hurricanes in the USA, 1900-92. Describe the pattern. How do you account for this pattern?

3 Explain why hurricanes in the USA are concentrated in the period between June and November (Figure 8.15).

4 Why does the Saffir-Simpson scale pay so much attention to mobile homes and piers?

5 Why does flooding of escape routes and coastal areas occur up to four hours before the arrival of the centre of the storm?

6 Why do strong west winds reduce hurricane activity in the USA?

Figure 8.17 A possible El Nino effect – flash-flooding in Peru

Although scientists have made great progress in predicting the occurrence and effects of El Nino they still do not know what causes its appearance or its strength. However, it appears to be increasing in frequency and strength, raising suspicions that it may be related in some way to global warming.

Inset 8.4
Hurricanes and tornadoes

Tropical cyclones, hurricanes and typhoons are all tropical depressions (low pressure systems) which develop over warm seas. The name varies – hurricanes in the USA and Caribbean, typhoons in Japan. By contrast, tornadoes develop as intense low pressure systems over a relatively small area of land (see pages 83 to 84). Any intense low pressure system can cause a storm surge (pages 57 to 60) as water levels are raised by 10 cm for every drop of 10 mb during a storm. So the surges in England in 1953 can be related to low pressure systems, rather than a hurricane (tropical storm).

The series of tornadoes that swept across Arkansas, Tennessee and Kentucky in 1998, for example, left eleven people dead and over 100 injured. Nashville was declared a disaster area and the US government provided funds to redevelop the area.

TORNADOES

Tornadoes are among the most violent storms on the surface of the earth. The Great Plains region of the central United States experiences about 70% of the tornadoes that occur on earth. US tornadoes typically move from south-west to north-east at speeds of up to 100 kmph (62 mph), with rotating wind speeds sometimes in excess of 500 kmph (310 mph) (Figure 8.22 on page 85). The most severe tornadoes are indeed ferocious (Figure 8.21 on page 85) – 1% of US tornadoes are responsible for over 70% of all deaths from tornadoes.

The optimum conditions for tornadoes to occur in the USA are provided when these factors occur simultaneously (Figure 8.18):

- a fast northerly flow of humid air from the Gulf of Mexico that has temperatures in excess of 24°C at the ground
- a cold, dry air mass moving from Canada or out from the Rocky Mountains at speeds in excess of 80 kmph
- jet-stream winds racing east at speeds in excess of 384 kmph.

The warm, moist Gulf air lifts upward, forming a strong updraft that is sheared and spun at mid-levels by the fast-moving polar air and then twisted in another direction at its upper levels by the jet stream. The corkscrew motion is enhanced by vertical movements of air: warm rising on the leading side, with cool air descending on the trailing side. Once formed, tornadoes derive additional energy from electrical discharges of lightning within the clouds and from latent heat released by heavy rainfall at the cloud's front.

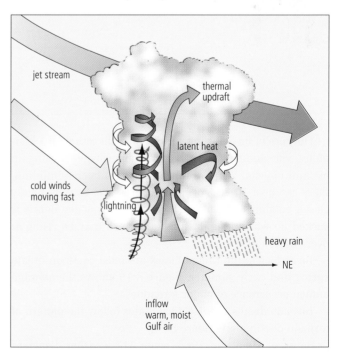

Figure 8.18 Components of a tornado, USA - general direction of travel is north-east

Source: Eagleman, J., Severe and unusual weather, 1983, Van Nostrand Reinhold, New York

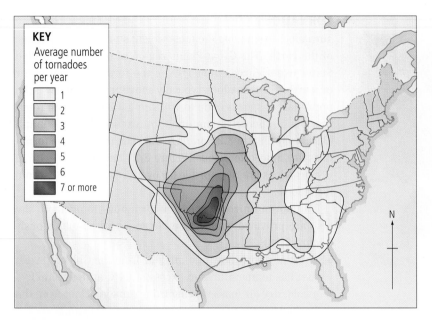

Figure 8.19 *Average annual occurrence of major tornadoes in the USA, 1953-80*
Source: Abbott, P., 1996, Natural disasters, W. C. Brown

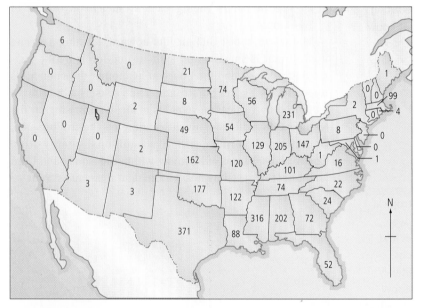

Figure 8.20 *Distribution of tornado deaths in the USA, 1953-80*
Source: Abbott, P., 1996, Natural disasters, W. C. Brown

The core of the whirling vortex is usually less than 1 kilometre wide and acts like a giant vacuum cleaner sucking up air and objects. When a tornado passes over a building, there can be a 10-20% drop in air pressure, causing tightly closed buildings to explode. Some of the exploded debris is sucked up with the updrafting air, which may be rising at over 160 kmph.

Tornadoes in the United States are most common in late spring and early summer. Figure 8.19 shows the average annual occurrence of major tornadoes.

Tornado deaths in the United States follow the pattern of tornado distribution (Figure 8.20).

Between 1965 and 1985, some 517 weather disasters were officially declared by the United States Federal Government and they killed over 4000 people. Every year 25-35 major weather disasters occur in the USA, causing deaths, damage to crops and property, disruption to transport and homelessness. However the death toll from tornadoes is lower than in past generations. Earlier warnings are now broadcast and people are better prepared.

QUESTIONS

1 Under what conditions do tornadoes form?

2 Describe the distribution of tornadoes in the USA, as shown in Figure 8.19.

3 Choose a suitable cartographic technique to show the number of deaths caused by tornadoes in the USA, 1953-80 (Figure 8.20).

4 What relationship is there between the distribution of tornadoes and the number of deaths? How do you explain this?

Inset 8.5
The Super Outbreak, April 1974

1974 was an exceptional year for tornadoes – producing the Super Outbreak of 3rd and 4th April. The weather scene on 2nd April 1974 included:

- a cold front spreading snow in the Rocky Mountains
- a low-pressure system moving east
- increasingly humid air over the 20°C water of the Gulf of Mexico
- a strong polar jet stream with a bend flowing from Texas to New England
- a dry desert air mass coming from the south-west attracted to the low-pressure system.

As the dry, desert air mass moved toward the Mississippi River, it overrode the moist Gulf air, forming an **inversion layer** that trapped unstable moist air below.

On 3rd April, all five weather systems came together. The unstable, moist air from the Gulf of Mexico began bursting up through the inversion layer, forming huge anvil-shaped thunder clouds that were set spinning by the other converging air masses. In 16 hours, 147 tornadoes occurred in 13 states. The destruction wrought by the Super Outbreak was overwhelming (Figure 8.21).

- 335 people killed
- 1200 people hospitalised
- over 7500 houses destroyed
- over 6000 houses severely damaged
- 2100 mobile homes destroyed
- over 4000 farm buildings destroyed
- 1500 small businesses destroyed or severely damaged
- 27 600 families suffered significant losses.

Figure 8.21 *Damage from the Super Outbreak tornadoes*
Source: Abbott, P., 1996, Natural disasters, W. C. Brown

F-0	under 72 mph	light
F-1	73-112	moderate
F-2	113-157	considerable
F-3	158-206	severe
F-4	207-260	devastating
F-5	over 261	incredible

Figure 8.22 *Fujita Wind Damage Scale*

SUMMARY

We experience 'weather' every day, and for most of the time we can either ignore it or take it for granted. However, in certain places and at certain times, 'normal' weather patterns are disrupted and we experience intense storms and gales. In the UK we are lucky – we do not experience regular storms as we have seen in the USA (and Bangladesh in Chapter 6). Severe storms, wherever they occur, create a range of hazards – high wind speeds, flooding, storm surges, landslides and so on. Places which do not normally experience strong storms (such as the UK and the gale of 1987 or north east USA and tornadoes) are affected more when the event strikes. Moreover, as we saw in Chapter 6, Coastal hazards, many poor communities cannot afford the necessary protection.

QUESTIONS

1 Under what conditions do either **(a)** hurricanes or **(b)** tornadoes occur? Why are they considered hazards? Use examples to support your answer.
2 Explain how a typical mid-latitude depression develops. Describe and explain the weather conditions experienced during the passage of a typical depression.
3 Explain why the Great Gale of 1987 caused so much damage in southern Britain. Why did the 1990 storm, which was slightly less intense cause more damage?

Extended (Project) work

Write your own case study of a low pressure system. You should collect information from a variety of sources:

- school weather system
- television weather reports
- local library
- local press for any details of damage
- the Meteorological Office
- Meteorological fax for daily weather charts (contact the Met Office on 01344 420242 for a regional netfax number)
- national newspapers.

BIBLIOGRAPHY AND RECOMMENDED READING

Abbott, P., 1996, *Natural disasters*, W. C. Brown
Burt, T. and Coones, P., 1990, *Winds of change*, Geography Review, 3, 5, 22-8
Coones, P. et al., 1987, *The Great Gale of 16 October 1987*, Geography Review, 1, 3, 6-10
Gregory, K., 1989, *Impact of the October 1987 storm*, Geography Review, 2, 4, 13-6
Musk, L., 1988, *Weather systems*, CUP
Slattery, M. and Burt, T., 1997, *The 1995 Atlantic Hurricane season*, Geography Review, 10, 3, 12-7
Salmond, J., 1994, *Hurricanes: a predictable phenomenon?*, Geography Review, 8, 1, 17-22

WEB SITES

Hurricane Andrew –
    http://geology.usgs.gov/program/marine/hurricane
Hurricane Fran –
    http://covis.atmos.uiuc.edu/guide/html/fran.html
National Hurricane Center –
    http://nhc-hp3.nhc.noaa.gov
National Weather Service's Tropical Cyclone Products –
    http://www.nhc.noaa.gov/products.html
TORRO: tornado and storms –
    http://.www.zetnet.co.uk/oigs/torro
WeatherNet's Tropical Page –

Chapter 9
Drought and desertification

In a number of chapters we have seen how flooding is a major hazard which causes widespread death and destruction. Floods are frequently very visible, short-term events, but not always. By contrast, drought is a long-term process, a 'creeping hazard' which occurs gradually and, in most cases, is not very newsworthy. Yet one-third of the world's population is affected by drought. In addition, some of the worst cases of drought and desertification are in developed countries which seem unable, or unwilling, to cope with the hazard.

WHAT IS A DESERT?

A large proportion of the world's surface experiences dry conditions (Figure 9.1). Semi-arid areas are commonly defined as having a rainfall of less than 500 millimetres per annum, while arid areas have less than 250 millimetres and extremely arid areas less than 125 millimetres per annum. In addition to low rainfall, dry areas have variable rainfall. For example, annual rainfall variability in a rainforest area might be 10%. This means, for example, that where the annual rainfall is about 2000 millimetres, in any one year the rainfall could be between 1800 millimetres and 2200 millimetres. As rainfall total decreases, variability increases. For example, areas with an annual rainfall of 500 millimetres have an annual variability of about 33%; in such areas rainfall could range from 330 millimetres to 670 millimetres. This variability has important consequences for vegetation cover, farming and the risk of flooding (Figure 9.2).

Arid conditions are caused by a number of factors. The main cause is the global atmospheric circulation. Dry, descending air associated with the **sub-tropical high pressure** belt is the main cause of aridity around 20°-30° N (Figure 9.3 a). In addition, distance from sea, **continentality**, limits the amount of water carried across the land by winds (Figure 9.3 b). In other areas, such as the Atacama and Namib deserts, cold off-shore currents limit the amount of condensation moving into the overlying air (Figure 9.3 c). Other arid conditions are caused by intense rain shadow effects, where wet air passes over mountains and loses its

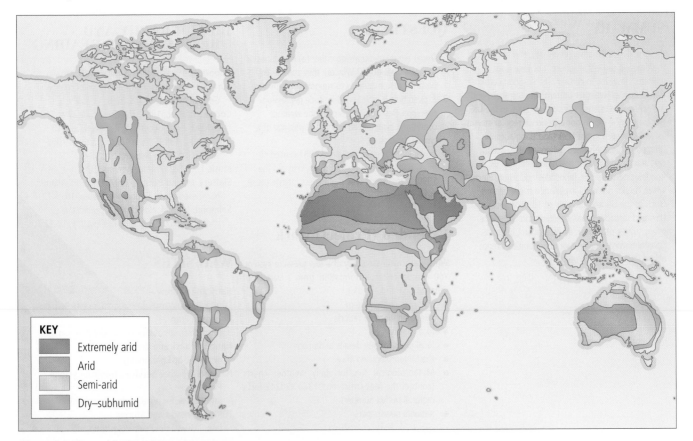

KEY
- Extremely arid
- Arid
- Semi-arid
- Dry–subhumid

Figure 9.1 The world's dry regions
Source: after UNEP, 1992

moisture, leaving the area in the lee of the mountain dry, for example, the Patagonian desert (Figure 9.3 d). A final cause, or range of causes, is human activity; many activities have given rise to the spread of desert conditions into areas previously suitable for agriculture. This is known as **desertification** and is an increasing problem.

Figure 9.2 *Satellite image of centre pivot irrigation in, New Mexico, USA*

Figure 9.3 *The causes of aridity:* **(a)** *sub-tropical high pressure belts,* **(b)** *continentality,* **(c)** *cold off-shore currents,* **(d)** *the rain shadow effect*

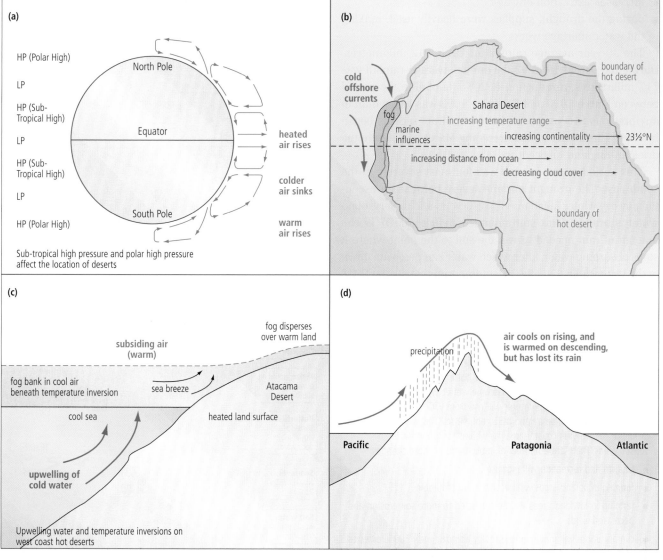

1 Describe the location of the world's dry areas as shown on Figure 9.1.

2 Briefly explain why there are deserts on the west coast of southern Africa and the west coast of South America.

DROUGHT IN THE UK

Drought is an extended period of dry weather leading to conditions of extreme dryness. Absolute drought is a period of at least 15 consecutive days with less than 0.2 millimetres of rainfall. Partial drought is a period of at least 29 consecutive days during which the average daily rainfall does not exceed 0.2 millimetres. In large parts of the UK there were periods of absolute drought in 1988-92.

The drought in the UK between 1988 and 1992 was caused by a number of factors:

- low summer and low winter rainfall
- during the drought, the summers were also much warmer and drier, especially in the south and east of Britain – this increased losses due to evaporation and transpiration (evapotranspiration)
- increased extraction of water
- during the drought, supplies were heavily used, making the water shortage worse.

The 30-year average rainfall for UK is 912 millimetres. During the period 1988-92 the annual average rainfall was 717 millimetres, a reduction of 20%. Rainfall in the period between March 1990 and February 1992 was lower than in any previous two-year period since accurate records began in 1767. The seven months preceding March 1992 were the driest in England this century.

This period of low rainfall was felt most severely in the south east. The drought became severe because an exceptionally dry winter failed to refill reservoirs and underground water storages. The soil-moisture deficit (SMD) is the amount of rain needed to wet the soil to the point where it stops absorbing water, after which water can percolate down to the water table. Usually the autumn rains satisfy the SMD. However in the south east between 1988 and 1992, SMDs continued until early winter and, in some areas, to the following spring.

By 2050 London's climate will be similar to that of Bordeaux today. The south and east of the UK will become hotter and drier whereas the north and west of the country will become wetter, with more frequent flooding. Average UK temperatures will rise from 9°C to 10.6°C, and global sea levels will rise by about 35 centimetres. This will cause problems in low-lying coastal areas as well as for groundwater in coastal areas. There are a number of implications of these changes:

- tourism and recreation will increase
- farming in upland areas will become more profitable
- farming in lowland areas will be subjected to more soil erosion and decreased yields
- climatic zones will move northwards by approximately 300 kilometres
- increased drought will lead to increased building subsidence
- there will be more storms and flooding.

Figure 9.4 The UK's changing climate
Source: Nagle, G. and Spencer, K., 1997, Sustainable development, Hodder and Stoughton

During the winter of 1991-2 the replenishment of underground water in the chalk hills, the region's most important source of water, was less than 15% of normal and some areas received nothing at all. In East Anglia, groundwater levels fell by up to eight metres, the lowest levels ever recorded. When the rains finally came in 1992, they were so intense that water ran off the surface rather than percolating to the water table.

Low rainfall was not the only problem. The long, hot summers of 1989 and 1990 brought record rates of evaporation of water from the soil. In a typical year, rainfall is 650 millimetres over south-east England but 550 millimetres of this is lost to evaporation. In 1989 only 475 mm fell – all of which was lost to evaporation.

The chance of drought in the UK is increasing as the climate becomes warmer (Figure 9.4). Its effects will vary across the country – some of which can be seen as beneficial but others could be disastrous (Figure 9.5).

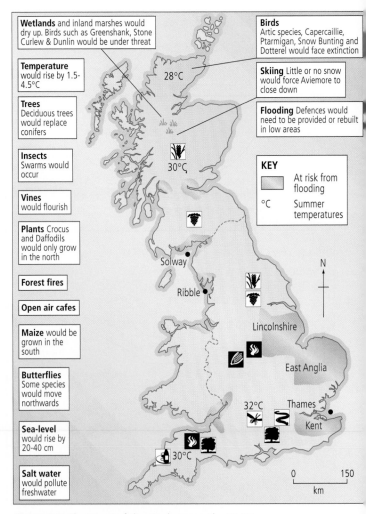

Figure 9.5 The impact of climatic change on the UK. Warmer temperatures? Less soil moisture in summer (more evaporation)? Fewer frosts? Smaller proportion of precipitation falling as snow? More forest fires? Flooding from a rise in sea level?
Source: Nagle, G., 1998, Geography through diagrams, OUP

Drought can be managed in a number of ways. Water supplies can be transferred, recycled and increased through a programme of reservoir building. However, as well as expanding supplies, better management and use of existing resources is needed. This involves more than short-term steps, such as hosepipe bans, but also long-term measures such as the installation of domestic meters, reduction of leakages, and introduction of campaigns to promote more economical use of water in industry, including farming, and in the home.

HAZARDS IN DRY AREAS

There are a variety of hazards which affect dry areas. These include:

- flooding of valleys, alluvial fans and plains (playas)
- increased soil erosion and gulleying
- surface subsidence due to water abstraction
  In areas where water is abstracted there is a reduction in pressure underground and the land may sink. This has already been experienced in London (see Chapter 13)
- sedimentation or deposition of river sediments
  In some areas, lower rainfall will lead to lower river flows, and consequently more deposition. This will reduce water quality, and make it murkier and less attractive for many plants and animals. It will also make the water less useful for irrigation, navigation and drinking
- landslides and rockfalls
  These are caused by weathering on rock faces (see Chapter 4). This prises open joints and cracks, and causes rocks to fall from the cliff face
- salt weathering.

The problem of flooding is significant because of the use of valleys and flood plains for settlement and farming. Stream flow in dry areas is seasonal; the dangers from flooding are due to a combination of:

- high velocities (Figure 9.6)
- variable sediment concentrations, some of which is quite large and can cause quite serious erosion
- rapid changes in the location of channels.

According to some geographers, semi-arid areas (variable but relatively low rainfall, relatively little vegetation cover) experience the highest rates of erosion and run-off (Figure 9.7). When it rains, a high proportion of rain hits bare ground and compacts it, causing high rates of overland run-off. The type of agriculture being practised directly affects

Figure 9.6 *A flash flood*

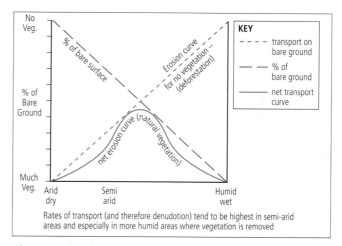

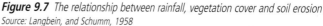

Figure 9.7 *The relationship between rainfall, vegetation cover and soil erosion*
Source: Langbein, and Schumm, 1958

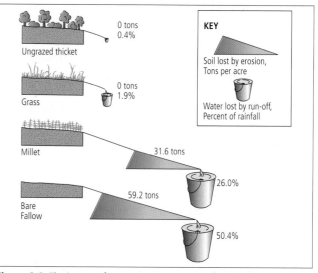

Figure 9.8 *The impact of vegetation type on run-off and soil erosion*
Source: Grove, A., 1989, The changing geography of Africa, OUP

the rate of soil erosion and amount of overland run-off (Figure 9.8). Under intense conditions (high rainfal combined with bare soil) this causes gulley formation. Gulleys are very narrow, very steep channels. For example, they may be a 5 metre incision in the landscape. They are formed by intense downward erosion by a stream or river. By contrast, in areas with very high rainfall, such as rainforests, the vegetation intercepts much of the rainfall and reduces the impact of rainsplash, and areas which are completely dry do not receive enough rain to produce much run-off.

Salt weathering is a major hazard in dry areas due to its ability to weaken engineering structures very rapidly. When temperatures rise above around 26°-28°C, sodium sulphate NA_2SO_4) and sodium carbonate (NA_2CO_3) expand by 300%. Also, when water evaporates, salts are left behind. In these ways, joints, cracks and weaknesses can be attacked by salt.

QUESTIONS

1 Study Figure 9.7 which shows the relationship between rainfall, vegetation cover and erosion.

a) Why is there limited erosion in areas where rainfall is very low?

b) Why is there limited erosion in areas where rainfall is very high?

c) Why are there high rates of erosion in areas with about 500 millimetres of rain per annum?

2 Figure 9.8 shows the effects of crop type on run-off and erosion. Describe what happens when scrub land (ungrazed thicket) is used for either pastoral agriculture (grass) or arable agriculture (millet). Describe and explain the effects of the removal of vegetation on run-off rates and erosion rates.

DESERTIFICATION

Desertification has been defined as the development of desert-like conditions in areas that were once green. It includes the spread of desert conditions as well as the intensification of desert conditions. Four elements, sometimes called 'the 4 Ds', have been identified in the process of desertification:

- **drylands** – 'susceptible to experiencing full desert conditions if mismanaged' – this is a climatic definition which implies fragility
- **degradation** – 'a reduction or destruction of the biological potential' – this is usually associated with unsound human practices such as overgrazing, deforestation, trampling, and overproduction
- **drought** – two or more years with rainfall substantially below the mean
- **desertification** – the combination of human and climatic variables which leads to the irreversible decline of the land.

Human induced climatic change can also be added to the list. In practical terms, desertification is a sustained decline in the yield of useful crops from a dry area, and environmental changes, such as declining vegetation cover, a drying soil containing less organic content, and increased soil erosion by wind and water. Although desertification is mostly

associated with semi-arid areas, it can take place in areas where intensive agriculture leads to a reduction in the availability of moisture. It occurs in EMDCs, such as Spain, the USA and Australia, as well as ELDCs countries such as Zimbabwe, Upper Volta and Botswana.

As well as determining the causes of desertification, it is also important to answer other questions. For example:
- is desertification irreversible?
- is it a long-term problem (or just a short-term blip)?
- what can be done about it?

There is still much uncertainty concerning the causes of desertification (Figure 9.9)

Myth	Reality
Desertification affects one-third of the world's land area	Such data are inaccurate, with problems separating natural variations from human actions
Drylands are fragile ecosystems that are highly susceptible to degradation and desertification	Drylands are more resilient than first supposed and are well-adapted to cope with and respond to disturbance
Desertification is a primary cause of human suffering and misery in drylands	Social problems may be due to political mismanagement rather than drought and desertification
Western aid bodies such as the UN are needed to solve the problem of desertification	Much evidence indicates that traditional human systems have evolved to cope with environmental disturbance

Figure 9.9 *Desertification – elements of uncertainty*
Source: Nagle. G. and Spencer, K., 1997, *Advanced geography revision handbook, OUP*

Among natural causes of desertification, climatic change – either natural or human-induced, is likely to be the main reason. Other natural changes could be:
- river capture, which could reduce the amount of water in an area
- changes in solar output
- variations in the earth's atmosphere due to increased levels of dust, volcanic ash and so on
- changes in the amount of polar ice and the effect this has on the reflection of solar energy.

One extreme view is that desertification is entirely the result of human activity. This view holds that overgrazing and the misuse of resources are the key elements. The argument for this view is that if the cause of desertification were natural it is likely that the desert would spread evenly along its margins. At present, however, desertification is taking place in a sporadic or scattered way, with small, isolated areas of degraded land appearing. This suggests that desertification at present is spread not by natural processes but by human pressures in localised areas.

A wide range of human activities can lead to the spread of desert conditions. These include the effects of over-grazing and trampling by pastoralists's animal herds, woodcutting, urbanisation, mining, tourism, the introduction of exotic plant and animal species, and even irrigation, by reducing the strength of soils. (Too much water makes the soil more mobile, and it can leach valuable chemicals or small particles which help bond the soil.) The relationship between these causes is highly complex, and likely to be self-perpetuating.

Pastoralists and desertification

Pastoral nomads are subsistence farmers who move with their herds in accordance with the rainy season and the availability of grazing. Some tribes may travel 800 kilometres each year. Pastoral nomads include the Hausa, Fulani and Moors of West Africa, the Pokot and Masai of East Africa and the Bedouin of Arabia.

During very dry spells they may concentrate their herds near bore holes (wells) and oases. This invariably increases the pressure of trampling on the vegetation (although this is partly offset by the natural manuring by the herds.)

The pastoralists need a certain number of cattle for subsistence and much of the land on which they live has low rainfall and is therefore sparsely vegetated; the sparse vegetation therefore comes under intense pressure. If a plant is grazed so much that most of the greenery is removed, photosynthesis may be reduced to a point where the plant dies. Grazing pressures are further intensified when pastoralists increase herd size in response to short-term variations in rainfall; in the long-term this strategy decreases the vegetation cover, reduces the soil moisture storage and intensifies the risk of overland run-off.

The problem of soil erosion is particularly severe around water holes, where the effects of trampling by herds can devastate the land (Figure 9.10). The first casualty is the

vegetation. Some animals are very selective grazers and will only eat the sweeter, more palatable species of vegetation. Concentration of herds around water holes reduces the cover of sensitive species and leaves a sparse cover of hardier, less palatable species, so the proportion of bare ground rises. Run-off and erosion rates increase as the proportion of bare ground increases. Animal hooves then pound and puddle the surface. In dry conditions, soil and plant litter (decaying remains) are broken down by hooves, to a size where they are easily eroded by the wind. When the rains come, the remaining dust may help to seal off the surfaces as an impermeable crust which reduces the infiltration capacity of the soil. Less infiltration and a lower surface roughness lead to increased run-off, erosion and a decline in water holding capacity. In addition, pounding in wet areas reduces infiltration in sites close to water courses because the soils are made impermeable.

The effects of trampling and over-grazing vary with soil type. On sandy soils, infiltration might not be as affected by pounding; on silt and clay soils there is a large decline in infiltration capacity.

However, there is some doubt over the impact of animals trampling. This arises through the nature of vegetation in deserts and semi-arid regions. Because of the low and variable rainfall, vegetation cover varies over a short-term (before and after a storm), mid-term (seasonal) and long-term (annual, decadal). Although animals trample and reduce vegetation near water holes they enrich the soils with nutrients in their faeces and urine. This allows for the recovery of plants once the herds have been moved away.

The collection of wood for fuel and construction can have similar effects. Around any semi arid small town or village, wood is collected for burning, and building, for example Duagadougou in Burkina Faso. Around some towns the zone without trees is commonly 30 kilometres; around Dakar, in Senegal, it is 300 kilometres.

It is possible to take measures to reduce the effects of desertification (Figure 9.11 on page 92). Measures include:
- fencing to keep livestock under control and preserve water sources
- improvements in herd quality, with higher milk yields and a better saleable value
- afforestation using native species
- carriage of water to stock rather than vice-versa.

Figure 9.10 The impact of animal herds near a water hole – the tracks left by the herds are clearly visible

Cause of desertification	Strategies for prevention	Problems and drawbacks
Over-cultivation	• Use of fertilisers: these can double yields of grain crops, reducing the need to open up new land for farming • New or improved crops: many new crops or new varieties of traditional crops with high yielding and drought resistant qualities could be introduced • Improved farming methods: use of crop rotation, irrigation, and grain storage can reduce pressure on land.	• Cost to farmers • Artificial fertilisers may damage the soil • Some crops need expensive fertiliser • Risk of crop failure • Some methods require expensive technology and special skills
Over-grazing	• Improved stock quality: through vaccination programmes and the introduction of better breeds – yields of meat, wool, and milk can be increased without increasing the herd size • Better management: reducing herd sizes and grazing over wider areas would reduce soil damage.	• Vaccination programmes improve survival rates, leading to bigger herds • Population pressure often prevents these measures
Deforestation	• Agroforestry: combines agriculture with forestry, allowing the farmer to continue cropping while using trees for fodder, fuel and building; trees protect, shade and fertilise the soil • Social forestry: village-based tree-planting schemes involve all members of a community • Alternative fuels: oil, gas and kerosene can be substituted for wood as sources of fuel.	• Long period of growth before benefits of trees are realised • Expensive irrigation and maintenance may be needed • Expensive; special equipment may be needed

Figure 9.11 *Measures to combat desertification*
Source: Nagle, G. and Spencer, K., 1997, Advanced geography revision handbook, OUP

DESERTIFICATION IN THE SAHEL

The Sahel region in Africa is the area to the south of the Sahara. It accounts for nearly 20% of the African landmass. The Sahel stretches for some 5000 kilometres and ranges from 300 kilometres to 1000 kilometres wide (Figure 9.12). Up to 100 million people live in the area which has a rainfall of between 125 millimetres and 600 millimetres per year.

Desertification has increased with population growth in the Sahel – the population there doubled between 1965 and 1983. Pressure on marginal land increased and agriculture in wetter areas intensified. Soil water levels declined; at the same time rainfall decreased (Figure 9.13). This led to widespread drought and famine. Malnutrition was widespread, and disease spread rapidly throughout the malnourished population. Food production dropped dramatically as crops could not be grown, nor was there enough forage for cattle, sheep and camels. The 1968-73 drought in the Sahel was a catastrophe – up to 250 000 people and 3.5 million cattle died.

However, conditions have not been monitored in detail and there are no reliable estimates of desertification which go back a long time. Thus, some geographers consider that there is not enough data or reliable long-term data to support the idea that desertification is taking place. They argue that it is, or may be, a short-term phase, which will, or may, change. The impact of global warming could make these areas wetter. Indeed, the 1991 El Nino season has seen widespread floods in Sudan – a normally dry area. However, by the same token, it is too soon to say that the process of desertification is over in these areas. The sobering point is that while some argue over definitions, the lives of millions are affected by drought, and perhaps, desertification.

QUESTIONS

1 What is desertification? Why is it a problem?

2 Explain **two** misconceptions in the desertification debate.

3 Study Figure 9.11 which shows measures to combat desertification. Which of the strategies for prevention offers the best chance of success? Justify your answer.

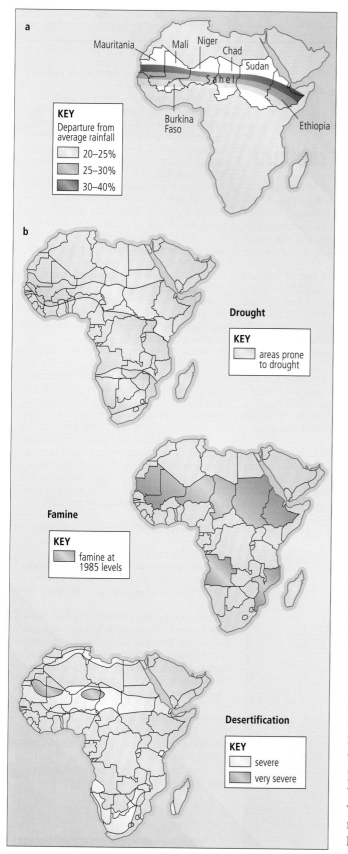

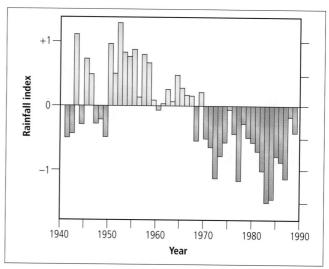

Figure 9.13 *Changing rainfall totals over the Sahel, 1940-90*
Source: Robinson, A., 1993, Earthshock, Thames and Hudson

QUESTIONS

1 Describe the pattern of rainfall in the Sahel as shown in Figure 9.13.

2 Describe the relationships between drought, desertification and famine as shown in Figure 9.12 b). For any **two** of these three features explain how they are related to each other.

DESERTIFICATION IN EMDCs

There is a common misconception that desertification only occurs in developing countries. This is not true. In fact, some of the worst cases of desertification are found in the developed world and relate to inappropriate types of farming.

The USA Dust Bowl

In the USA during the 1870s and 1880s, as the settler population moved westwards across the great plains of central USA, they experienced a period of above average rainfall and adopted farming practices which were more appropriate for a wet area rather than a dry area. In this century, drought affected the great plains on average every twenty years but it was not until the 1930s that the seriousness of the situation was noticed. In the mid-1930s, 19 states were hit by severe storms, and tons of topsoil, loosened by mechanized farming, was swept into the air, creating the Dust Bowl. The wind erosion seriously affected large areas and individual households, by destroying them, or covering them with sand. Farmers in the area continued to use farming practices that required large volumes of water, such as centre-pivot irrigation schemes to enable the production of wheat (see Figure 9.2). However, these schemes required the removal of trees and wind breaks so that the revolving booms could rotate and they have depleted the store of water in the underlying aquifer. The US government is keen to reduce the effects, and is preventing farmers from over-exploiting the land.

Figure 9.12 (a) *The Sahel and **(b)** the relationship between drought, desertification and famine in Africa*
Source: Binns, A., ed, 1994 People and environment in Africa, Wiley

Desertification in Australia

Australian
crisis as farmland turns to desert

Australia is losing precious soil on a scale that is compared to the desertification of Ethiopia, causing an economic disaster that now costs $Aus 2 billion (£1 billion) a year. In some areas cattle can no longer graze, crops will not grow and people are abandoning farms.

But far more serious is the actual loss of the land, which will cost a further $Aus 2.5 billion to repair where possible. More than half of Australia's farming country is in need of treatment and scientists estimate that 4.3 million hectares of that is on the verge of becoming permanent desert unless immediate steps are taken to stop an irreversible process of land degradation. Already there are places where it has been left too late and farming activity has gone forever.

The problems have been known about for many years. Yet only now, as the economic damage becomes clear, is notice being taken in a year of growing criticism from environmentalists at home and abroad.

The government's own scientists say that years of neglect, coupled with a refusal to change inappropriate farming practices, have brought Australia to the edge of a man-made disaster.

Variously described as the 'Aids of the Earth' and 'environmental holocaust', desertification is recognised as the largest single problem facing the country and one which demands a dramatic rethinking of land management.

'Land degradation, in a general sense, is probably costing Australia $Aus 2000 million a year,' Dr. David Smiles, Chief of Soils Division of the Commonwealth Scientific and Industrial Research Organisation told *The Times*. Dr Smiles is leading research into the extent of the problem and is trying to establish and promote the cures.

The problem lies in the great age and fragility of the Australian landscape and the devastating toll that 200 years of European settlement has taken on the relatively fertile soil. Dust samples have been found in New Zealand and over the Tasman Sea.

'The black soil plains of New South Wales and Queensland are basalt flows 10 to 15 million years old whose net loss was millimetres in thousands of years,' Dr Smiles explained. 'If you look at what we've managed to do in 200 years – the very deep gullies, wrought by the clearing of vegetation, cultivation, grazing and construction – you realise the immense pressure we have put on the land.'

Although comprising less than one-third of the total land area, Australia's non-arid zones are home to 98% of the population and have to support all its grazing and crop production. Forty per cent of good crop land is badly eroded. Ninety per cent of rural New South Wales needs treatment.

Victoria is particularly badly hit by salinity, with 650 000 square kilometres affected in varying degrees. In Queensland 28 000 square kilometres of land need repair after water erosion. Most of South Australia is prone to wind and gully erosion. In western Australia, salinity and coastal erosion is the problem.

In a country where 40 per cent of exports are produced directly from the soil, one economic equation stands out. Every tonne of grain is now estimated to 'cost' 13 tonnes of precious top soil. Agriculture is likened to mining, where soil is removed permanently.

'We are mining both the carbon and the nitrogen from our landscapes,' Dr Smiles explained. 'The land was protected by its own vegetation. Its removal and removal of the nutrients of millions of years before cultivation represents catastrophic devastation. Only now are we dimly perceiving the problems.'

These include erosion, salinity, acidification, the effects of introduced animals, and chemical pollution from agro-chemicals. Environmentalists like Dr David Bellamy of Britain and Dr David Suzuki of Canada are among those who have voiced strong criticism in Australia this year.

'Modern Australia is an ecological disaster, characterised by a squalid history of greed, short-sightedness and ignorance,' Dr Suzuki said after a recent trip here. That such remarks are given front page prominence in Australia's newspapers is an indication of the need for change.

But persuading farmers to reduce cattle stocks or not to break up the soil for cultivation is not easy. Therefore, a surprising development is the coming together this year of environmentalists known as the 'greenies' and farmers whose usual hostility has given way to dialogue to help save the situation.

The economic effects of environmental problems, however, are not only limited to the soil. The 'greenhouse effect' also threatens Australia's lucrative ski-fields in the New South Wales mountains.

As a result, environmental issues are moving to the centre stage of Australian politics.

Figure 9.14 *Desertification in Australia*
Source: The Times, 1988

QUESTIONS

1 Read the article in Figure 9.16 and answer the following questions.

a How much land in Australia is becoming desert? What will it cost to repair this?

b Why has desertification occurred in Australia?

c Why have the last 200 years been so crucial in causing soil loss?

d What percentage of Australia is arid. How many people live there?

e List **four** problems that are facing Australian farmers. How much of Australia's exports come from the soil?

f Why is it proving difficult to get Australian farmers to change their ways?

SUMMARY

In this chapter we have seen how drought and desertification affect a large proportion of the earth's surface and population. Their impact is likely to increase as the population increases and as climate changes. Moreover, there is great uncertainty about its cause, its extent, and what can be done to improve the situation. As we have seen, it affects developed countries as well as developing countries. Its impact on the world's greatest food producers, such as the USA and Australia, is very serious. Some developed countries, geared up to large-scale, intensive commercial agriculture seem unable to cope with the threat of desertification. By contrast, many traditional communities are much better able to adapt and cope.

QUESTIONS

1 What are the main causes of aridity?
2 With the use of examples, describe the possible causes of, consequences of, and solutions to, the problem of desertification.
3 Explain why flooding is a problem in semi-arid areas.

BIBLIOGRAPHY AND RECOMMENDED READING

Agnew, C., 1995, *Desertification, drought and development in the Sahel*, in Binns, A., (ed.) People and environment in Africa, Wiley
Grove, A., 1989, *The changing geography of Africa*, Oxford
Middleton, N., 1995, *The global casino*, Arnold
Robinson, A., 1993, *Earthshock*, Thames and Hudson
Thomas, D. and Middleton, N., 1994, *Desertification: exploding the myth*, Wiley

WEB SITES

CSIRO – The greenhouse effect –
    http://www.dar.csiro.au/pub/info/greenhouse.html
Amazing environment organisation web directory –
    http://www.webdirectory.com
Global warming on the World Wide Fund for Nature –
    http://www.panda.org/climate/road2kyoto/scorecard/score.htm

Chapter 10
Air quality

In this chapter we look at a hazard which affects over 1.6 billion people each year, poor air quality. In the UK, for example, one child in seven now suffers from asthma and this problem has been linked with poor air quality; in some developing cities poor air quality has been connected to reduced achievements in school. The chapter begins with a comparison of air quality in the developed world and the developing world. We look at the main pollutants and then examine air pollution in Athens, Moscow, Cubatao (Brazil) and Oxford. Air quality in Mexico City and London are discussed in detail in Chapter 13, which focuses upon the range of hazards found in these two cities.

AIR QUALITY: AN OVERVIEW

Poor air quality affects 50% of the world's urban population, a total of about 1.6 billion people. Each year several hundred thousand people die due to poor air quality and many more are seriously affected. The problem is increasing due to increasing population growth in urban areas, industrial development and an increase in the number of vehicles world-wide. In Europe, three-quarters of cities with populations over 500 000 have poor air quality (Figure 10.1).

The world's population is growing by about 95 million people each year. This increases the demand for energy, transport, heating and so on. Increasingly, more and more people are living in urban areas. In 1970, 3.7 billion people (37% of the world's total) lived in urban areas. This increased to 5.3 billion (43% of the world's total) in 1990 and is estimated to reach 6.25 billion (50%) by 2000.

In developing countries, population growth is very rapid and cities have less resources to cope than cities in developed countries. Overcrowding is widespread in many cities throughout the world but reaches alarming proportions in cities in the developing world. In London, for example, population densities reach as high as 4000 people per square kilometre. By contrast, densities per square kilometre are 24 000 in Cairo, 34 000 in Mexico City and 88 000 in Calcutta. In many developing countries, indoor air pollution is also high due to the burning of fuelwood and paraffin for cooking and heating. Up to 700 million people in the developing world are thought to be at risk of high levels of indoor air pollution.

Figure 10.2 shows a model of air quality and levels of economic development. Poor countries have weaker economies so investment in pollution control is minimal. Instead, such countries favour industrialisation and the use of cheap, inefficient energy resources, such as lignite and low grade coal,

Figure 10.1 *Poor air quality in Athens*

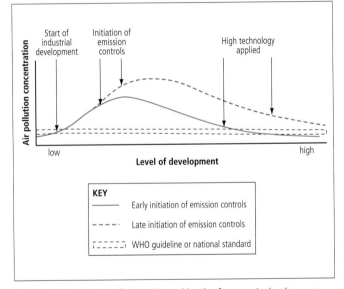

Figure 10.2 *A model of air quality and levels of economic development*
Source: Middleton, N., 1995, The global casino, Edward Arnold

as a source of energy. By contrast, rich countries – which may have gone through a process of deindustrialisation – have the capital and the technology to tackle air pollution.

One of the major sources of pollution is motor vehicles. At present, developing countries account for about 10% of the world's motor vehicles and about 20% of the world's cars. This proportion will increase greatly over forthcoming decades. In particular some countries, such as India and China, are expanding their car industries as a key part of their economic development. Cars and other vehicles in developing countries tend to be less fuel-efficient and produce more pollution because they are older, poorly serviced and lacking in clean, environment-friendly technology. In addition, roads are often in a poor state and this reduces the quality of vehicles quickly. In many cities there are limited funds to tackle urban air pollution. City planners have to balance the demands for clean air against the needs for housing, education, employment, health and so on. Environmental issues are rarely top of the agenda.

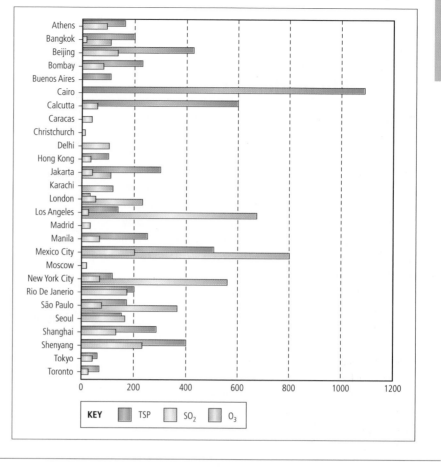

Figure 10.3 *Levels of air pollution in selected cities*
Source: Elsom, D., 1996, Smog alert, Earthscan

KEY ■ TSP ■ SO₂ ■ O₃

QUESTIONS

1 Figure 10.2 shows a model of air pollution and level of economic development. Describe how levels of pollution vary with levels of economic development. Suggest **two** contrasting reasons why developed countries have lower levels of pollution than developing countries.

2 Explain why environmental concerns are more likely to be tackled in developed countries rather than developing countries.

3 Study Figure 10.3 which shows levels of air pollution in selected cities. Which cities have the highest levels of **(i)** TSPs (total suspended particulate matter) **(ii)** sulphur dioxide (SO₂) and **(iii)** ozone (O₃)?

AIR POLLUTION AND HEALTH

Air pollution has been linked with health problems for many decades. People most at risk include asthmatics, those with heart and lung disease (such as bronchitis, emphysema and angina), infants and pregnant women. This accounts for 20% of the population in the developed world and an even higher proportion in the developing world. The death rate from asthma in developed countries has increased from 40% to 60% in recent decades and is now one of the most common causes of hospital admissions for children. In June 1994, for example, there was a significant outbreak of asthma in the UK, when high pressure conditions were experienced, favouring high levels of ozone.

In the USA it is estimated that the costs related to air pollution are about US$40 billion each year. This is made up of US$16 billion in health care costs and a further US$24 billion in lost productivity and absenteeism.

The main air pollutants in urban areas are sulphur dioxide, fine suspended particulates (smoke, dust, PM_{10}s), nitrogen oxides, carbon monoxide, VOCs (volatile organic compounds, such as the carcinogenic (cancer-forming) benzene), ozone, acid aerosols, lead and other metals. The emissions of pollutants are quite staggering – in 1990 global emissions of sulphur dioxide were 99 million tonnes, suspended particulates 57 million tonnes, nitrogen oxides 68 million tonnes, and carbon monoxides 177 million tonnes.

In the UK, the Clean Air Acts of 1956 and 1968 introduced controls on emissions of smoke, grit and dust from domestic and certain industrial sources and controls on chimney heights, and empowered local authorities to designate smoke control areas. Since then there have been significant changes in the sources of pollutants, with motor vehicles an increasingly important source. Fuel combustion is the major source of sulphur dioxide (SO_2), oxides of nitrogen (NO_x), carbon monoxide (CO), carbon dioxide (CO_2), hydrogen chloride (HCl), hydrocarbons and heavy metals; it is predicted that by 2030, there will be up to one billion vehicles worldwide emitting these pollutants. Industrial processes, storage and use of chemicals are also sources of these compounds.

QUESTIONS

1 Give **three** contrasting reasons why young children, joggers and the elderly are at increased risk of air pollution.

2 What diseases are linked to air pollution?

Inset 10.1
Air quality guidelines

In 1987 the World Health Organisation (WHO) published advisory guidelines for ambient concentrations of a wide range of organic and inorganic compounds. The guidelines are set some way below the minimum concentrations at which adverse effects have been observed. Others are set at levels above which adverse ecological effects on health have been observed, on the basis that some plants display a higher sensitivity to air pollutants than humans. For some carcinogenic compounds, such as benzene, WHO were unable to recommend a safe level.

SUMMER AND WINTER SMOG

Air pollution episodes are now classified by the Department of Health into one of three categories:

1 Summer smog – ozone (O_3), respirable particulates (PM_{10}) and to a lesser extent nitrogen dioxide (NO_2)
2 Vehicle smog – nitrogen dioxide (NO_2), respirable particulates (PM_{10})
3 Winter smog – high levels of SO_2 during high pressure weather systems

Summer smog, also known as photochemical smog, occurs on calm, sunny days when photochemical activity leads to ground–level ozone formation. Ozone is formed when complex reactions take place between nitrogen oxides and VOCs in sunlight. Other compounds are formed, including acid aerosols (sulphates, sulphuric acid, nitrates and nitric acid), aldehydes, hydrogen peroxide and PAN (peroxacetyl nitrate). This process may take a number of hours to occur, by which time the air may have drifted into surrounding suburban and rural areas, causing higher levels of ozone pollution outside the city centre. The effect of excessive amounts of ozone is to cause stinging eyes, coughing, headaches, chest pains, nausea and shortness of breath, even in fit people. Asthmatics may experience severe breathing problems.

In city centres, it is nitrogen dioxide rather than ozone that is likely to be the main pollutant, and the cause of vehicle smog. Vehicles emit nitric oxide as well as nitrogen dioxide. The nitric oxide is converted (oxidised) into nitrogen dioxide by reactions with oxygen and ozone. This process uses up some of the ozone, and thus reduces the ozone concentration over city centres.

Winter smogs are associated with cold, high pressure conditions, temperature inversions and high rates of sulphur dioxide emission due to increased heating of homes, offices and industries. Also, in cold conditions vehicles operate less efficiently and need more time to 'warm up'. This releases larger amounts of carbon monoxide and hydrocarbons. Urban areas surrounded by high ground are especially at risk from winter smogs. This is because cold air sinks down from the surrounding hills, reinforcing the inversion. This occurs on a range of scales from relatively minor, albeit noticeable smog, such as in Oxford, to very serious smog, such as in Mexico City.

Poor air quality often persists for many days. This is because it is associated with high pressure conditions which generally prevail for at least a few days. In some climates, notably Mediterranean climates, stable, high pressure conditions persist all season so poor air quality can persist for a number of months.

Although smogs occur under certain atmospheric conditions (namely high pressure), human activity (the emission of pollutants) is responsible for the environmental hazard.

THE POLLUTANTS

Sulphur dioxide and smoke

Sulphur dioxide (SO_2) is released by the combustion of sulphur-containing fuels such as coal, smokeless fuel and oil. Highest emissions are around power stations and major industrial areas. Sulphur dioxide aggravates asthma; coughs, bronchitis and chest illnesses increase as the levels of sulphur dioxide rise. In Paris, for example, between 1987 and 1992, heart attacks increased as daily sulphur dioxide levels rose. However, the correlation is not straightforward since increased sulphur dioxide levels are also related to increased levels of acid aerosols and it could be the acid aerosols that lead to the rise in heart disease.

Sulphur emissions are falling – oil and natural gas emit very small amounts, although diesel emits more. Since the 1960s, SO_2 emissions declined to under 4 million tonnes in 1983. The increasing use of sulphur-free fuels such as natural gas, lower industrial energy demand and energy conservation have contributed to the decline particularly in urban areas (see Figure 10.4). Emissions by industry other than power stations have declined from 27% of the total in 1980 to 19% in 1990. However, it is still a problem in many eastern European countries where coal is widely used. In addition, pollutants can be transported large distances. This

QUESTIONS

1 What are stable, high pressure conditions? Why are pollution episodes associated with high pressure conditions?

2 Explain **two** ways in which a smog may be formed.

means that pollutants from as far as eastern Europe can drift over to western Europe. Some of the worst pollution in Europe is in the 'Black Triangle' (also known as the 'sulphur triangle' and 'triangle of death') which consist of the northern Czech Republic, southern Poland and part of the former East Germany. Here pollution is on a par with the London smog of the 1950s – the 'pea-soupers' (see Chapter 13 Hazards in London and Mexico City).

Figure 10.4 Return of the pea-souper

Black smoke (suspended particulate matter) consists of fine particles (mainly carbon) from incomplete combustion of fossil fuels. Black smoke emissions are produced mainly from road transport and from homes. Road transport accounted for almost 46% of total emissions in the UK in 1990, with buses and heavy goods vehicles contributing most. Homes accounted for 33%, mostly from coal burning. Black smoke emissions have declined by just under 20% since 1980. Emissions from domestic sources have halved since 1980 whilst those from road transport have doubled.

Sulphur dioxide and smoke pollution from coal burning have largely disappeared from the UK. In Northern Ireland and Ireland, however, turf and peat are still burnt as fuel, hence in winter high levels of sulphur dioxide are still found. Occasional episodes of 'poor' concentrations of sulphur dioxide continue to occur, particularly in Belfast – 27 days in 1990 (Figure 10.5).

Little data is available for developing countries, but the study of Mexico in Chapter 13 on pages 119–21 provides a useful case study.

Respirable particulates

Respirable particulates (PM_{10}s) are very fine suspended particulates, less than $10\mu m$, which are small enough to penetrate deep within the lungs. PM_{10} pollution may cause 60 000 deaths each year in the USA and 10 000 in the UK, mostly among the elderly and those with respiratory diseases.

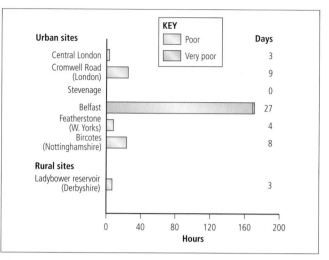

Figure 10.5 Number of days with unacceptable levels of SO_2 in selected areas of the UK, 1973-89
Source: Department of the Environment, 1992, The UK environment, HMSO

Increased levels of PM_{10}s are associated with higher levels of morbidity (illness) and mortality (death). Even quite low concentrations lead to decreased lung capacity and increased heart and respiratory diseases, including asthma. There is no safe limit and even a few PM_{10}s could enter the lungs and pass through the alveoli into the bloodstream.

Levels of PM_{10} are increasing because of the increased use of diesel (it is a more efficient and economical fuel). Diesel emits fine particulates, including benzene, which can penetrate the lungs. Other sources of PM_{10}s include smoke and lead.

Carbon monoxide

Carbon monoxide emissions have increased by over 30 per cent since 1980; high levels of carbon monoxide are found at busy road junctions especially at rush hour (Figure 10.6). The highest levels occur in underground car parks, enclosed bus stations and tunnels. Levels can also be very high inside the vehicle. Carbon monoxide reduces the absorption of oxygen by haemoglobin, increases heart stress, and affects the nervous system. Unborn children are especially at risk.

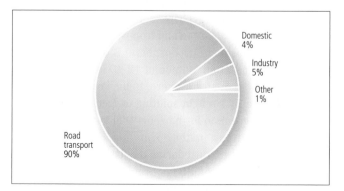

Figure 10.6 Sources of carbon monoxide emissions in the UK, 1990
Source: Department of the Environment, 1992, The UK environment, HMSO

Nitrogen oxide

There are many types of nitrogen oxide. They can cause coughs and sore throats, and can have an effect on asthmatics and people with bronchitis. Nitric oxide (NO) and nitrogen dioxide (NO_2) (jointly termed NO_x) are gasses formed in the combustion process from the nitrogen present in fuels and from the oxidation of nitrogen in air. The effects of oxides of nitrogen are varied. High concentrations can reduce plant growth and cause visible damage to sensitive crops, add to acid deposition, and play a part in the formation of ground-level ozone.

Extensive surveys in 1986 and in 1991 showed that average UK concentrations of nitrogen dioxide increased by 35% over the period, mainly as a result of increased emissions from traffic. High concentrations usually occur in winter, particularly in calm, cold weather when pollutants are trapped close to the ground by temperature inversions.

Volatile organic compounds

Volatile organic compounds (VOCs) include a large number of chemical compounds which are able to evaporate into a gas and take part in chemical reactions. They include methane, ethane and alcohol. VOCs contribute to the formation of photochemical gases such as ozone. Some VOCs cause minor complaints such as skin and eye irritations, coughing and sneezing; others, such as benzene, are carcinogenic. The source of benzene in urban areas is from petrol exhausts and the evaporation of petrol during refuelling.

Data available for developed countries show that emissions of volatile organic compounds have risen gradually during the 1980s and are now 4% higher than 1980. Emissions from processes and solvents accounted for half of total emissions and road transport just over 40%.

Ozone

There are no significant direct emissions of ozone into the atmosphere so it is referred to as a secondary pollutant. Ozone is formed by a complex series of reactions between nitrogen oxides and volatile organic compounds (VOCs) in the presence of sunlight. There is an important distinction between stratospheric ozone and tropospheric ozone. Ozone in the lower atmosphere (troposphere) is different from the ozone layer found at an altitude of 12-40 kilometres in the upper atmosphere or stratosphere. In the lower atmosphere ozone is formed by sunlight splitting oxygen molecules into atoms which regroup to form ozone. Due to the role of photochemical reactions in the formation of ozone, ozone concentrations are greatest during the day, especially during warm, sunny, stable conditions. Above 20°C reactions are accelerated and ozone formation increases.

Ozone can harm lung tissues, impair the body's defence mechanism, increase respiratory tract infections, and aggravate asthma, bronchitis and pneumonia. Even at relatively low levels, coughing, choking and sickness increase. The long-term effects include the premature ageing of the lung. Children born and raised in areas where there are high levels of ozone can experience up to a 15% reduction in their lung capacity.

Background levels of ground-level ozone have risen substantially over the last century. There is evidence that the preindustrial ground-level concentrations of ozone in the UK were typically 10-15 parts per billion (ppb). These have increased over the past 100 years so that current annual mean concentrations are approximately 30 ppb over the UK. The number of hours of 'poor' ozone concentrations tend to increase from the north to the south of the country (Figure 10.7). Concentrations can rise substantially above background levels in summer heat waves when there are continuous periods of bright sunlight with temperatures above 20°C and light winds. Once formed, ozone can persist for several days and can be transported long distances; pollution transported with continental air masses plays a significant role in UK ozone episodes.

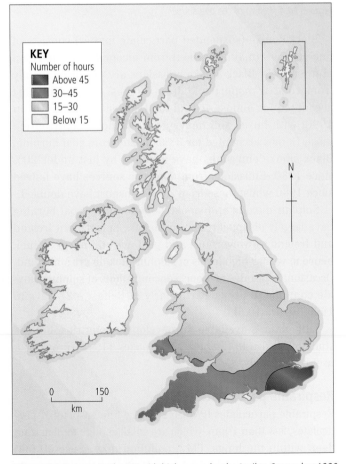

KEY
Number of hours
- Above 45
- 30–45
- 15–30
- Below 15

Figure 10.7 *Areas in the UK with high ozone levels, April to September, 1990*
Source: Department of the Environment, 1992, The UK environment, HMSO

Lead

The main source of lead in urban areas is leaded petrol. The effects of lead include increased blood pressure, heart attacks, kidney disease, reproductive damage and ultimately brain damage. Children are most at risk – high rates of lead affect the nervous system and can cause behavioural problems, reduced concentration levels and poor performance at school.

Levels of lead in the UK and USA have fallen by over 90% since the 1980s following the reduction in the permitted lead content of petrol and the introduction of unleaded petrol. Unleaded petrol was introduced not only because of the health implications but also because cars with catalytic converters needed lead-free petrol.

In developing countries, levels of lead are still very high. This is especially so in Mexico City, Cairo and Bangkok. In Bangkok, for example, it is estimated that high lead levels cause up to 500 000 cases of high blood pressure (hypertension), leading to 400 deaths each year. Similarly, in Mexico City it is estimated that up to 70% of children have their development affected by high lead levels.

QUESTIONS

1 Describe the trends in SO_2 levels in the UK as shown in Figure 10.5 (page 99). How do you account for this pattern?

2 Study Figure 10.5 (page 99) which shows levels of SO_2 for selected places in the UK. Which location has the worst level of SO_2? Why should this be the case?

3 What are the main sources of carbon monoxide as shown in Figure 10.6 (page 99)?

4 Study Figure 10.7. Describe and explain the geographical variations in high ozone levels.

CITIES AND AIR POLLUTION

We now look at a number of examples of cities with a variety of air pollution problems. These include:

- Cubatao – a developing world city
- Moscow – a city where the main forms of energy have changed
- Athens – a very polluted city which shows contrasts between industrial pollution, and vehicle/residential pollution
- Oxford – a small city whose physical geography adds to the problem of air quality.

The city of Los Angeles, USA, has some of the worst air quality in the world. On average, unhealthy air quality (as defined by the WHO) is recorded on more than one-third of days each year and in 1988 it was recorded on nearly two-thirds of the days.

Most cities in ELDCs are suffering from severe air pollution due to:

- rapid population growth
- increasing manufacturing and energy production
- expansion in the number of motor vehicles.

Population growth and increasing manufacturing industry are not characteristic of EMDC cities; the growth in motor vehicles is common to both.

In Bangkok (Thailand) air pollution and poor visibility are increasing problems. Bangkok has a population of about 7 million people and there are over 2 million cars in the city. About 12% of the city's population suffers chronic respiratory problems and air pollution causes about 1200 deaths annually. The World Bank has calculated that by the age of seven the average child has lost 4 IQ (intelligence quotient) points due to the high levels of lead in the atmosphere.

Cubatao, Brazil

Up until the 1980s, Cubatao had the reputation for being the most polluted place in the world. This had resulted from rapid industrial development without any environmental legislation. Petrochemicals, fertilisers, cement, steel, chemicals and paper were produced in an attempt to industrialise. The result was catastrophic: the infant mortality rate increased rapidly and nearly 50% of the population had some form of respiratory complaint.

In the 1980s the Brazilian authorities began to tackle the problem by the installation of pollution control equipment and the closure of manufacturing plants during pollution episodes. Although it has not 'solved' the problem it has gone some way to decreasing it. Airborne lead levels decreased from 1.6 mg/m³ in 1978 to 0.3 mg/m³ in 1983, folowing widespread adoption of ethanol fuel.

Air pollution in Athens – the 'nefos'

The Greek word 'nefos' means cloud and illustrates the fact that in Athens air pollution is very visible. In Athens, large concentrations of aerosols (solid particles) form a cloud that is turned yellow by the presence of nitrogen dioxide; the cloud reduces visibility in Athens considerably. During a typical pollution episode, the main concentration of non-black (other) particulates is over the industrial areas west of the city (Figure 10.8 on page 102); over the city centre black smoke (carbon-based particles from diesel vehicles and heating) is the main pollutant. Figure 10.9 on page 102 shows the levels and composition of particulates in the nefos over central Athens and over the industrial district. The graph shows a decline in levels of black smoke but no decline in non-black particles. Black smoke levels have declined due to tighter control of burning coal in residential areas, and resticted use of cars (based on their registration numbers) on certain days. By contrast, non-black smoke pollution remains high, largely as a result of manufacturing activities.

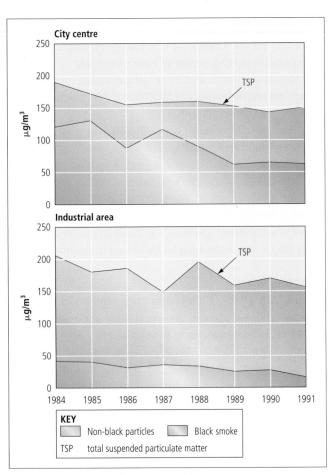

Figure 10.8 *Characteristics of the nefos, Athens, 1984-91*
Source: European Environment Agency, 1995, Europe's environment, EEA

Changing patterns of air quality in Moscow

Moscow is a good example of the changing patterns of air quality resulting from changes in fuel consumption away from oil and coal to natural gas. Emissions of sulphur dioxide and smoke have dropped dramatically since the late 1980s. This has resulted in reduced concentrations of smoke (Figure 10.9), although they are still higher than WHO guidelines. Levels of lead have also decreased, the result of a government control on the sale of leaded petrol. By contrast, concentrations of nitrogen dioxide have risen significantly since the mid 1980s, as a result of increased vehicle traffic and power generation.

Air quality in Oxford

Oxford is situated at the confluence of two rivers, the Thames and the Cherwell. On calm days, cold air drains into the valley and there is often a temperature inversion (colder air below, warmer air above). This stops air from rising and hence pollutants are trapped within the temperature inversion. Episodes of pollution are becoming more frequent, and people are sometimes advised not to enter the city at certain times unless their visit is essential, as the air quality is so poor.

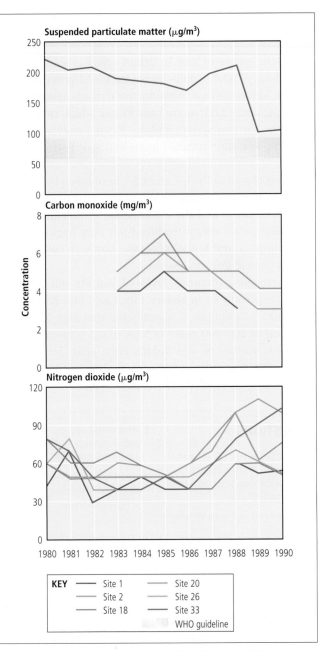

Figure 10.9 *Changing patterns of air quality in Moscow, 1980-90*
Source: European Environment Agency, 1995, Europe's Environment, EEA

The Oxford Transport strategy aims to improve the environment in the heart of Oxford by the introduction of restricted traffic movements through the central area. This will lead to the closure of some of the main streets, e.g. High Street, to through traffic and to the pedestrianisation of others, e.g. Cornmarket.

The pollutants, monitored hourly, and plotted relative to safety thresholds, are:

- nitric oxide
- nitrogen dioxide
- carbon monoxide
- sulphur dioxide
- respirable particulates
- ozone.

SUMMARY

In this chapter we have focused upon air quality in urban areas. We have seen how developed countries and developing countries differ in terms of the scale and nature of the problem, and the ability to cope with the problem. The association between poor air quality and health is strong, and there is also an effect on mental development. Our examples have shown how factors such as industrial development, concentrations of vehicles and high pressure conditions combine to produce serious pollution episodes.

QUESTIONS

1 What are the causes, consequences and potential solutions to poor air quality in urban areas?
2 How does the hazard of poor air quality in urban areas differ between developed and developing countries? Use examples to support your answer. (N.B. Readers may find it useful to compare the case studies of London and Mexico City in Chapter 13 with the cities discussed in this chapter.)

Extended (Project) work

Contact your local Environmental Health Department. Ask them for details concerning the monitoring of air quality. For example:
• which pollutants are monitored?
• which sites are monitored?
• what are the results?
• how do you explain these results?

The Department of Environment Air Quality Bulletin system provides daily air quality bulletins, forecasts and associated health advice. This material is available on a free telephone service (0800 556677) and is carried by some national and local newspapers and on Ceefax (page 196). Information can also be found on Ceefax (pages 410-415), Teletext (page 106) and Freephone Air Quality Information Service on 0800 556 677.

BIBLIOGRAPHY AND RECOMMENDED READING

Elsom, D., 1996, *Smog alert: managing urban air quality*, Earthscan
European Environment Agency, 1995, *Europe's environment*, EEA
Department of the Environment, 1992, *The UK environment*, HMSO
Department of the Environment, 1997, *The environment in your pocket*, HMSO
Middleton, N., 1995, *The global casino*, Edward Arnold
Oxford City Council, 1995, *Oxford Air Watch Annual Report*, 1995

WEB SITES

HMI Pollution –
http://www.open.gov.uk/doe/epsim/index/html
Manchester Air Quality –
http://www.doc.mmu.ac.uk.aric/arichome.html
Westminster City Council: air quality home page –
http://www.wcceh.gov.uk/

difficult working conditions, there are gaps in the container, which are regularly monitored for radiation leakage. More than a decade later, in September 1997, the European Union pledged US$115 million to make the sarcophagus safe after an international team had found it in urgent need of repairs to prevent radiation leakage.

Outside the plant, the nearby town of Pripyat was closed within hours and the residents were advised to stay indoors. It was later decided to evacuate everybody from within a 30-kilometre radius of the reactor. After the evacuation, decontamination work began. Within the evacuation zone, all soil to a depth of 15 centimetres was removed and all buildings in Chernobyl and Pripyat were cleaned. These measures were later found to be limited in their effect. To prevent the contaminated land being washed away, and to prevent radionuclides seeping into rivers and the Kiev reservoir, 140 dykes and dams were built. A large concrete wall was constructed around the plant, deep into the ground, to prevent radionuclides passing into the soil water and ground water. In addition, a channel was created to prevent contaminated water getting in to the River Dnepr and downstream into drinking sources. In 1997 the area around Pripyat was still an exclusion zone.

Further afield, the deposition of radioactive material varied. Many places had less than 1 kBq/m^2 whereas others had in excess of 100 kBq/m^2. (kBq/m^2 = one thousand becquerels/m^2, 1 becquerel = 1 disintegration per second.) This led to wide variations in the contamination of foods throughout Northern Europe.

Figure 11.4 The sarcophagus, Chernobyl

THE NUCLEAR HAZARD

At the end of 1995 there were 437 nuclear reactors in operation throughout the world. These accounted for 17% of the world's electricity needs and 6% of total energy needs.

In much of western Europe, its nuclear plants are ageing and need to be decommissioned (dismantled). However, the costs of decommissioning obsolete nuclear power stations are enormous. The long-term liability for all nuclear plants has been estimated at U$30-37 million. However there is so little experience of the process and the costs involved that these figures must be regarded as an estimate. Nuclear power in eastern Europe is largely produced by Chernobyl-type reactors, which do not meet western safety standards.

Japan's nuclear energy programme is unique among economically more developed countries (EMDCs). Nuclear power is at the forefront of its energy policy and the government intends to increase the amount of nuclear power as a percentage of all the power they produce. However, the nuclear industry in Japan faces a number of problems. There is increasing opposition because of fears over the safety of plant operations and waste disposal. In particular, the Kobe earthquake in 1995 increased public awareness of the hazards of a major nuclear disaster.

Most nuclear waste from Japan is shipped abroad and disposed of in the UK and France. Nevertheless, the amount of stored nuclear waste in Japan has almost doubled between 1990 and 1997 to over 5000 tonnes. Increasingly, much of this waste has been stored at Aomori, at the northern tip of Monshu, the main island. It was chosen because it is a remote area, isolated and underpopulated, and thought to be safer than other sites in Japan. Since the disaster at Kobe, all of Japan is now thought to be at risk. In 1995, a leak of three tonnes of non-radioactive material occurred at Monju, Japan's experimental fast-breeder reactor. Residents and critics felt that if the reactor could leak non-radioactive material, it could leak radioactive material too. Public opposition to Japan's nuclear strategy reached its peak in 1996 when residents in Maki turned down proposals for a new nuclear plant.

In the newly-industrialised countries (NICs) of Asia, such as China and South Korea, and the Ukraine, the growth of power-generating capacity is seen as a major factor in economic development and the concentration of new nuclear power plants is in these areas. China plans to increase its nuclear reactors from three in the mid-1990s to 11 in 2000. However, economic growth is not just dependent upon more power-generating capacity, but also on the more efficient delivery of output. Energy losses of 25-30% (electricity generated but not used), from all energy sources, are common throughout Asia, and in India they reach as high as 65%.

Radioactive dumping sites at sea

As Figure 11.5 shows, the UK is not immune to nuclear accidents and is also at risk from the dumping of radioactive material at sea. Material dumped at sea contains nuclear waste not only from the UK, but also from Japan. In 1997, the government revealed that radioactive waste had been dumped in at least eight previously unacknowledged sites in

Level	Description	Criteria	Example
7	Major accident	• External release of a large fraction amount of radioactive material. Such an event would have acute health affects, delayed health effects over a large area, and long-term environmental consequences	Chernobyl, 1986
6	Serious accident	• External release of radioactive material requiring emergency countermeasures	Kyshtym (Russian Federation), 1957
5	Accident with off-site risk	• External release of radioactive material requiring partial emergency measures • Severe damage to the nuclear facility – fire or explosion releasing nuclear material within the facility	Windscale, UK, 1957 Three Mile Island, USA, 1979
4	Accident without significant off-site risk	• External release of radioactivity resulting in the need for local food control • Significant damage to the nuclear facility • Overexposure of one or more workers causing a high probability of an early death	Windscale, UK, 1973
3	Serious incident	• External release of radioactive material • On-site events causing a health risk • Incidents which could lead to further accidents	
2	Incident	• A failure in safety procedure but no external risk • A worker is placed at risk; precautions need to be taken	
1	Anomaly	• Outside normal operating levels	

Figure 11.5 *The scale for international nuclear events*
Source: European Environment Agency, 1995, Europe's environment, EEA

the sea for four decades up to the 1970s. For example, during the 1950s, radioactive waste was dumped in a trench under shipping lanes in Beaufort's Dyke in the Irish Sea. In addition, a number of new sites were identified:

• Firth of Forth, off North Queensferry – scrap from a Ferranti radioactive valve manufacturing unit was dumped between 1954 and 1957
• North Sea – UK Time dumped sealed drums in 1949 and the 1950s
• explosives disposal site off the Isle of Arran – ICI dumped two radioactive anti-static devices before 1958
• Garroch Head on the River Clyde – material from a former radium factory dumped in 1963
• North Sea, beyond the Thames Estuary and in the Firth of Forth – liquid waste or sludge containing small amounts of radioactivity was dumped in the 1960s and early 1970s
• Liverpool Bay area – industrial sludges containing 'enhanced natural radioactivity' were dumped in the early to mid 1970s.

The Atomic Weapons Establishment at Aldermaston in Berkshire has been producing nuclear weapons for nearly 40 years. Radioactive by-products and contaminated equipment are stored on the site. In the mid-1980s the government recognised the problem of nuclear waste disposal and drew up plans to build three new facilities capable of storing 100 tonnes of nuclear waste each year. However, these facilities have not been built and it is likely that all storage space at Aldermaston will be filled by 2002.

Hiroshima, 1945

Of all technological disasters, war is the worst. One of the most harrowing examples of such disasters is the bombing of the Japanese cities of Hiroshima and Nagasaki in 1945. Before it was bombed on August 6th 1945, Hiroshima had been free from bombing. The decision to bomb the city was a deliberate US policy to see what effect the atomic bomb would have on a built-up area. When the bomb was dropped on Hiroshima, up to 75 000 people were immediately killed by the blast and fires that broke out. Many more died later as a result of radiation – the death toll is now estimated at 200 000 in total from the initial blast and illnesses related to the bomb. The thermal rays and the blast force destroyed all the buildings in central Hiroshima with the exception of the A-Bomb dome (Figure 11.6 on page 108). Over 60 000 buildings were totally burned or destroyed. A further hazard was radioactive rain – the rain brought down radioactive particles suspended in the air (Figure 11.7 on page 108).

Figure 11.6 The A-bomb dome

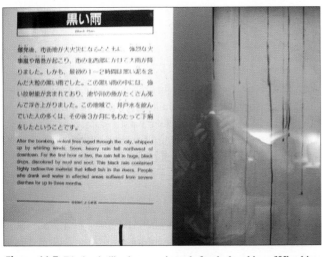

Figure 11.7 Black rain like that experienced after the bombing of Hiroshima

QUESTIONS

1 Study Figure 11.5 which classifies nuclear accidents and incidents. Where should the bombing of Hiroshima be placed? Justify your answer.

2 Give reasons why the plume of radioactive material travelled westwards across Europe after the Chernobyl explosion. How else might radioactive material be transported?

3 Why is the risk of a nuclear disaster in Japan so great? Suggest at least **two** reasons.

4 On a map of the British Isles, locate the dumping sites of radioactive material. Describe the distribution of radioactive dumping sites around the British coastline.

FIRE

Since early times, fire has been used for ritual, social and industrial purposes (pottery, forging), cooking, protection, war or aggression, heating and light. In addition, fire has been used to manipulate plant and animal communities:

- to clear land for agriculture, attract game and deprive game of cover
- to improve grazing by removing dead vegetation and encouraging new grass and faster growing herbs, at the expense of longer living woody trees
- to drive away wild animals.

Fire, started by humans, created the heathland and moorland ecosystems of Britain for example, as well as the savannas and temperate grasslands of the mid-latitudes. Much of Europe's heathlands was formerly forests, but burning and grazing have prevented regeneration.

Fire is a serious hazard in areas where there is a long dry season or where lightning is common. Other natural causes include fermentation of litter, and sparks caused by boulders hitting each other. Fires from natural causes also occur more frequently in semi-arid and savanna areas than temperate and cool temperate areas. In the USA, more than 50% of the fires are natural whereas in Australia and the south of France almost all of the fires are man-made, caused by arson, accidental damage or land management.

The temperature of a fire varies with the type of vegetation and the frequency of fire.

Forest fires are hotter than grassland fires because there is more dead organic matter. More frequent fires are less intense than rare fires, because there is a relatively small build up of inflammable material. Suppressing fires can lead to a build up of combustible matter, leading to greater temperatures and intensity. Land-use management practices can intensify adverse fire conditions. The air temperature of rare fires can reach 600-900°C!

Australian bush fires, 1994

Australia had a very dry period between October 1993 and January 1994 – so much so that the plant litter was very dry in areas around Sydney. The Australian bush fires of January 1994 were the result of a combination of factors: intense heat during the day (>40°C), for a number of days, causing plants to ignite later; lightning; littering of cigarettes; arson; and the dry weather, which made the vegetation extremely dry.

The fires at Royal National Park, Sydney, burned 98% of the vegetation, especially the small, young plants. Other effects included: air pollution; increased soil erosion; reduced water supplies; disruptions to communications networks; cuts to the electricity supplies.

However, the rate of regeneration was very rapid: by May 1994 there was much new growth and the ecosystem was showing signs of recovery.

Case study:
South-east Asian fires, 1997-8

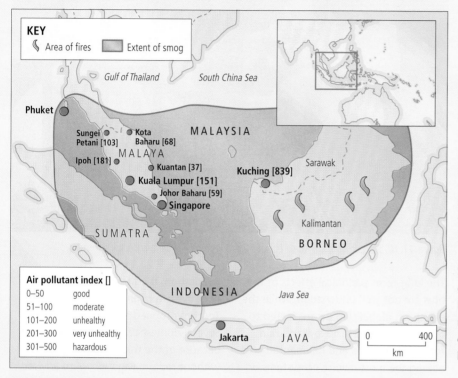

KEY

◖ Area of fires   ▨ Extent of smog

Gulf of Thailand   South China Sea

Phuket

Sungei ○   ○ Kota
Petani [103]   Baharu [68]

MALAYSIA

Ipoh [181] ○   MALAYA

○ Kuantan [37]   Kuching [839]   Sarawak

● Kuala Lumpur [151]

○ Johor Baharu [59]

● Singapore

SUMATRA   Kalimantan

BORNEO

Air pollutant index []

0–50	good
51–100	moderate
101–200	unhealthy
201–300	very unhealthy
301–500	hazardous

INDONESIA   Java Sea

● Jakarta   JAVA

0 — 400 km

Figure 11.8 South-east Asia and the smog
Source: Financial Times, September, 1997

During 1997 and 1998, forest fires raged across approximately 4.5 million hectares of rainforest and palm oil, tea, rubber and timber plantations on the Indonesian islands of Kalimantan and Sumatra. Thick smog created by the fires covered parts of Indonesia, Malaysia, Brunei, Singapore, the southern Philippines and southern Thailand (Figure 11.8), an area larger than western Europe. Up to 70 million people were blanketed by smog created by the fires (Figure 11.9). In places visibility was less than one metre!

Some of the fires were forest fires but others were caused by areas of peat burning. The peat, which is up to twenty metres deep, may be on fire to a depth of three metres deep in parts and could burn underground for decades.

The fires have had many effects. An Indonesian airliner crashed in thick smog on 26th September 1997, as it came in to land on the Indonesian island of Sumatra. All 234 passengers and crew on board were killed. Over 275 people have died from starvation in the Indonesian province of Irian Jaya, because their food supplies were burned, and the settlements were so isolated that it was impossible to get emergency relief to the inhabitants. Others on Irian Jaya have died from cholera caused by a lack of clean water – smoke, ash and soot made the water dirty.

In February 1998 satellites revealed 247 separate fires on Borneo alone. Many fires spread out of control because of the absence of rain during south-east Asia's dry season. This has been blamed on El Nino. The total cost of the disaster has been estimated at almost $2 billion.

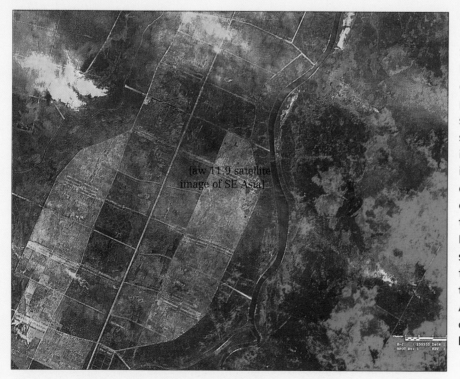

Figure 11.9 Satellite image of the smoke in south-east Asia

In the Malaysian territory of Sarawak, the indigenous communities were particularly affected. Living in remote forests, cut off from medical care or access to bottled water, they received very little help from the government or aid organisations. Schools in Sarawak were forced to close down; hospitals struggled to cope with the increase in the number of throat infections, diarrhoea, conjunctivitis and other eye problems.

Over 60 000 Malaysians and Indonesians, mostly children and the elderly, were treated for smog-related illnesses. The effect of the smog has been likened to smoking three packets of cigarettes each day. Some doctors claim that the effects are even worse – that the sulphide and carbon gases produced by the fires obstruct the airways and destroy the lungs (Figure 11.10).

Many of the Indonesian fires were started deliberately by plantation owners and those with logging interests as a cheap way of clearing the land for agriculatural use. The Indonesian government blamed 176 plantation companies for causing the fires, but has taken limited action against any of them; many of these companies have western customers, and it is a source of foreign exchange. For example, in 1996, the UK imported over 200 000 cubic metres of tropical timber from Indonesia, where over 1 million hectares of rainforest are lost to logging every year.

Figure 11.10 *Schoolchildren in Kuala Lumpur wearing masks for protection against smog*

The long-term ecological effects of the fires are not well understood, while the effects on global climate are feared to be very significant. The lowland rain forests of Sumatra and Kalimantan are among the most diverse ecosystems on earth. The fires could lead to a huge loss of biodiversity. The problem is increased because much of the forest lies on a bed of peat. Scientists have warned that up to 1 million hectares of peat swamp forest could be destroyed by the fires, and that peat fires which burn underground could take up to ten years before they go out. The effect of this would be to prevent seeds germinating and the lack of food would pass up through the food chain, possibly leading to the decline of such species as tigers, orang utangs and elephants.

Scientists fear that the uncontrollable fires which burnt 250 square kilometres (over 600 000 hectares) of south-east Asia will cause long-term climate disruption. The effect of the fire, especially if it continues to burn in the peatlands, could release huge amounts of carbon dioxide into the atmosphere, which could speed up global warming.

In addition, the fires have had a negative effect on economic activities. Tourism dropped almost immediately. Several domestic flights were cancelled because of the thick smog. Ships without radar navigation were advised not to sail in the Straits of Malacca, which separates Malaysia from Indonesia. Crop yields were down and many food exporting countries, such as Thailand and the Philippines, had to import coffee and rice.

The problems of fire in the region have been compounded by the El Nino effect (see Chapter 8, Storms and hurricanes, page 82) which was blamed for the drought in Asia in 1997 and the late arrival of the monsoon rains; reservoir levels have dropped and some have been contaminated by sea water.

SUMMARY

In this chapter we have looked briefly at technological hazards, and at one in particular, the nuclear hazard. The effects of nuclear power are immense. Whether it is used aggressively or as a means of energy production, nuclear technology has the capacity to destroy people and places on a vast scale. The cost of making nuclear structures safe is very expensive – we saw that progress at Chernobyl has been painfully slow since the accident in 1986.

Fire, one of the longest used elements of nature, remains both a hazard and a resource. It can be natural or man-made, and its results can be devastating. The case study of the south-east Asian fires show that short-term economic profits can seriously affect the long-term environmental health of a large area.

QUESTIONS

1 With the use of examples, describe and explain the term 'technological disasters'.

2 How safe is nuclear power? Support your answer, with the use of examples.

3 With the use of examples, explain how physical geography affects a technological disaster.

4 With the use of examples, describe and explain the causes and consequences of fire as a hazard.

Extended (Project) work

Accidents related to vehicles are one type of technological hazard. Contact the transport division of your local City Council or County Council. They should be able to provide you with a breakdown of traffic-related accidents. From these you can work out:

- cause of accident (car, lorry, motorbike, etc.)
- time of accident
- day of accident
- seasonal variations in the number and type of accidents
- location of accidents.

Analyse this data in relation to factors such as traffic density, type of road, speed limits, weather patterns. Other information can be obtained from your local police force, local newspaper or local library. This will allow you to build up a picture of a technological hazard for your district.

BIBLIOGRAPHY AND RECOMMENDED READING

Blunden, J. and Reddish, A., 1996, *Energy, resources and environment*, Hodder and Stoughton

DTI, 1993, *Development of oil and gas resources of the UK, 1992*, HMSO

European Environment Agency, 1995, *Europe's environment*, EEA

Mumsford, B., 1988, *The fuelwood trap*, Earthscan

Philip's Geographical digest annual, Heinemann

Wood, D., 1994, *Oil spills around the UK coastline*, GeoActive, 106

WEB SITES

Friends of the Earth –
http://www.foe.co.uk/

Greenpeace International –
http://www.greenpeace.org/greenpeace.html

Sea Empress oil spill –
http://www.swan.ac.uk/biosci/empress/empress.htm

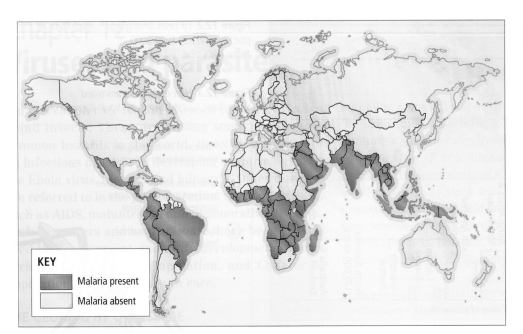

Figure 12.4 *The global distribution of malaria, 1992*

KEY

Malaria present

Malaria absent

As yet there is no universal vaccine. In southern Tanzania up to 80% of the children are infected with the disease by the age of six months, and 4% of children under the age of five die as a result of malaria. Pregnant women, travellers and refugees are also very vulnerable to the disease.

QUESTIONS

1 Study the map of the global distribution of malaria for 1992 (Figure 12.4). Describe the location of areas affected by malaria.

2 In what temperature range do the parasites in the mosquitoes thrive?

3 What kind of water do mosquitoes need to lay their eggs?

4 How might changing agricultural practices affect the distribution of malaria? Give at least **two** contrasting practices and effects.

5 There are over 3000 cases of malaria in Europe each year, and the number is increasing. Why should this be so?

Schistosomiasis

Schistosomiasis (also known as bilharzia) causes chronic ill-health. Up to 200 million people are infected with the disease and a further 600 million are at risk. It is transmitted in stagnant water by parasitic worms, called schistosomes (Figure 12.5). In water, worm larvae grow in the bilharzia snail (hence the alternative name for this disease, bilharzia). Worms develop within the snail, leaving the snail to find a human host. Female worms lay hundreds of eggs daily for up to five years.

The worms damage the intestine, bladder and other organs. Schistosomiasis kills 20 000 each year and also causes bladder cancer. In Egypt, for example, bladder cancer is the main cause of death in males under the age of 44 years. The disease is spread by large-scale dams and irrigation which increase the amount of stagnant water.

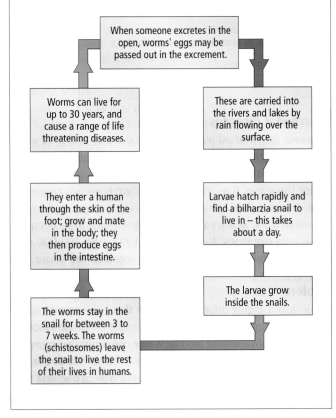

When someone excretes in the open, worms' eggs may be passed out in the excrement.

Worms can live for up to 30 years, and cause a range of life threatening diseases.

These are carried into the rivers and lakes by rain flowing over the surface.

They enter a human through the skin of the foot; grow and mate in the body; they then produce eggs in the intestine.

Larvae hatch rapidly and find a bilharzia snail to live in – this takes about a day.

The larvae grow inside the snails.

The worms stay in the snail for between 3 to 7 weeks. The worms (schistosomes) leave the snail to live the rest of their lives in humans.

Figure 12.5 *The bilharzia cycle*
Source: Nagle, G., 1998, Geography through diagrams, OUP

SUMMARY

In this chapter we have looked at diseases caused by viruses and parasites. Infectious diseases account for a staggering 17 million deaths each year, and it is expected that this number will increase. Much of the problem is related to population growth, overcrowding and unhygienic conditions. These are associated with conditions of poverty, which are widespread in developing countries. But there are also increasing numbers of infectious diseases in developed countries, notably TB. In addition, we have seen that new diseases have emerged, such as the ferocious Ebola virus.

QUESTIONS

1 Using an atlas, explain why schistosomiasis should be a problem in Egypt.
2 Study Figure 12.5 which shows the life cycle of schistomiasis. Suggest two contrasting ways in which the disease could be prevented.

Extended (Project) work

1 Visit your local library and look at the Medical Officer's Reports for selected years at regular intervals, such as 1871, 1881, 1891, 1901. How have the number of cases of different infectious diseases changed over that period? What explanations are given in the reports for outbreaks of disease, such as cholera epidemics in the nineteenth century?
2 Contact the infectious diseases unit at your local (regional) hospital and the Environmental Health Department of your local council. Ask them for available data on the type and number of cases of infectious diseases in your area. (But remember that patient confidentiality cannot be broken.) Try to build up a picture of infectious diseases in your area.
3 This chapter has focused on a small number of hazards. Using your school library or a local public library find out about the following pests and infestations:
• locusts
• potato blight
• onchoceriasis.

BIBLIOGRAPHY AND RECOMMENDED READING

Black, D. and Whitehead, M., 1992, *Inequalities in health: the Black Report (new edition)*, Penguin

Howe, G. M., 1976, *Man, environment and disease in Britain*, Penguin

Jones, K. and Moon, G.,1987, *Health, disease and society*, RKP

Learmouth, A., 1988, *Disease ecology*, Blackwell

Nagle, G., 1998, *Development and underdevelopment*, Nelson

World Health Organisation, 1996, *The World Health Report*, 1966, WHO

WEB SITE

World Health Organisation – http://www.who.ch/

Chapter 13
Hazards in London and Mexico City

In this final chapter we examine the nature of some of the hazards in two large cities, London and Mexico City. The two case studies highlight the multiple hazards that will exist in any one city. Although there are a number of stark contrasts between London and Mexico City, some of the hazards, such as air pollution and industrial disasters, are similar. Other hazards relate to specific site characteristics: London's low lying estuarine location makes it vulnerable to sea surges and high tides, whereas Mexico City's position close to a tectonic boundary makes it vulnerable to earthquakes.

LONDON

London has experienced a variety of hazards since the 1200s. Examples of hazards, and some of the measures to manage them, include:

- a Royal Decree in 1306 which banned the burning of coal in order to reduce air pollution
- the Great Fire of London in 1666 which burnt over 13 200 homes
- the Little Ice Age of the seventeenth century which caused the Thames to freeze over
- a boiler explosion in 1858 in the London Docks which killed over 2000 people
- the blitz in World War II which reduced much of London to rubble, especially its industries and residential areas in the densely packed inner city
- high tides and storm surges, for example in 1953
- smog, for example in 1955, 1991 and 1997 (Figure 13.1)
- hazardous waste - London currently produces 129 000 tonnes each year.

A detailed examination of these hazards reveals interesting patterns. For example, although more WWII bombs fell on suburban areas than on inner city areas, the more dispersed nature of the buildings in the suburbs reduced the spread of fire and most of the impact was felt in inner areas. The Battle of London, 'the Blitz', took place in 1940 and 1941. Some 360 raids were responsible for almost 30 000 deaths. The most severe raids took place in April and May 1941 and up to a quarter of all deaths took place in just four raids. The largest loss of life was on the 10th and 11th May when at least 1436 lives were lost. By contrast, most structural damage occurred on 29th and 30th December. Strong winds spread fires throughout the City and combustible materials such as books in publishers' premises, old churches and closely packed buildings provided materials to fuel the

Figure 13.1 *London's pea-souper smog, 1952*

fire. The bombs dropped during the war remain a potential hazard, as many unexploded bombs still remain buried in the ground.

Another hazard is much more long-term, and has been a threat for the last 10 000 years. London is increasingly at risk of storm surges. This is due to a combination of:

- rising sea levels (caused by the greenhouse effect and global warming)
- down tilting of the south of England (caused by the isostatic uplift of Scotland as a result of the end of the last glacial period)
- long-term subsidence (caused by the weight of buildings on the sediments of London).

As a result, the Thames Barrier was constructed in 1983 to protect London from high tides and storm surges.

Many other hazards are purely human in origin. Canvey Island is a chemical and oil refining complex on the banks of the Thames Estuary. The flammable material stored there, if ignited, could kill as many 18 000 people who live close to the works, and one report concluded that it constituted a 'severe public safety hazard'.

Air quality

In the 1950s London experienced severe smogs ('pea-soupers'). The pea-soupers were largely caused by unrestricted coal-burning in homes and industries – manufacturing industries and domestic fires spewed out masses of particulates and sulphur dioxide. The smog occurred under high pressure conditions, whereby low level temperature inversions trapped the pollutants near ground level. One of the worst smogs was between 4th and 10th December 1952 (Figure 13.1). Visibility was down to five metres, the fog had an acidity of 1.6, a thousand times more acidic than normal rainfall, and a level at which large-scale respiratory problems are caused. There were nearly 4000 deaths, especially among the elderly and those with pre-existing respiratory problems.

Such pea-soupers became rare for a number of reasons:

- the 1952 smog caused the government to introduce the 1956 Clean Air Act – financial assistance was given to households to convert to smokeless fuel
- houses gradually converted to oil, gas and electric heating
- deindustrialisation
- legislation reduced the sulphur content of oil to 1%.

For some decades it was believed that London's smogs were a thing of the past. London's SO_2 concentrations fell from about 300 $\mu g/m^3$ in the mid-1960s to below 50 $\mu g/m^3$ in the 1980s (Figure 13.2). However, in the late 1980s and early 1990s, although the causes were different, smogs returned. The main sources of pollution had changed: cars and other vehicles were the main source of particulates, carbon monoxide, nitrogen oxides and volatile organic compounds (VOCs). The worst winter smogs to occur in the 1990s were in December 1991. Under cold, high pressure conditions, levels of nitrogen dioxide peaked at 423 parts per billion (ppb), more than twice the WHO safe limit of 209 ppb. Over 160 deaths were attributed to the smog. In addition, levels of benzene (a volatile organic compound (VOC)) rose by as much as seven fold. Similar smogs, although not as intense, occurred in Manchester and Birmingham.

Since 1980, photochemical (summer) smogs have been more frequent in hot, high pressure conditions. Ozone levels of 100-150 parts per million (ppm) have been common, especially in suburban locations, exceeding WHO guidelines on a number of occasions. These smogs occur in suburban and rural areas throughout the South East region rather than inner London; over central London, the ozone is used up in the conversion of nitric acide to nitrogen dioxide, so ozone levels fall. The pollutants not only drift out of London

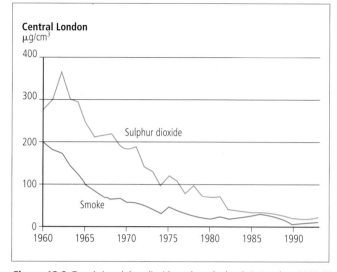

Figure 13.2 *Trends in sulphur dioxide and smoke levels in London, 1960-90*
Source: Energy Study, 1997, London Research Centre /Focus on London, HMSO

but are also blown over from the continent. On some occasions, such as May 1995, up to 50% of the ozone is from France and a further 25% from Germany.

The main reason for this increase in air pollution has been the increase in the number of cars on the road. Improvements to the road network have led to more cars on the roads and greater concentrations of cars in out of town sites. This is related to an increase in the number of facilities, such as hospitals, shopping centres and sports complexes, located further from residential areas and suburban centres. These facilities are much easier to access by car than by public transport. Other sources of pollutants are aeroplanes and power stations. Air traffic accounts for 3% of London's emissions of nitrogen oxides, and power stations on the Thames estuary are the main source of sulphur dioxide.

The Conservative government in the 1980s and 1990s attempted to reduce levels of pollution using a variety of methods:

- variable speed limits on the M25 to reduce the number and length of traffic jams
- Red Routes in London (on which stopping is not permitted) to reduce the amount of exhaust fumes given off
- pedestrianisation of shopping centres
- the reintroduction of trams, such as between Croydon and Wimbledon.

Nevertheless, there are still a large number of old vehicles in operation emitting large amounts of harmful gases.

QUESTIONS

1 How do the causes of smogs in the 1990s compare with the causes in the 1950s?

2 Study Figure 3.2. Describe the trend of sulphur dioxide levels. How do you explain this change?

3 Why are ozone concentrations greater in suburban areas than central areas, and nitrogen levels higher in central areas? (You may wish to look at Chapter 10 for a full discussion.)

London's groundwater

During the early part of the century, water levels in the chalk aquifer in north and central London fell owing to over-abstraction; this left a large volume of aquifer empty. Since the 1940s, abstractions have decreased so that in most parts of London, especially in the central area, water levels are now rising. Rising groundwater levels may pose a threat to foundations and tunnels constructed while levels were depressed.

The problem arises because there is a layer of chalk over London's groundwater system and a layer of clay above that in which most underground structures are embedded. Far less groundwater is used today because many of London's heavier industries have left the area in recent decades, particularly since the 1970s. The higher level of groundwater is causing the chalk and clay to buckle under the pressure.

Some parts of London are now at risk from rising water levels. The London Underground railway and other underground structures such as car parks are most at risk. The most badly affected area of the London Underground lies inside the route of the Circle Line – west from Tower Hill to Earl's Court, north to Paddington, and east to Liverpool Street. The City, Mayfair and Westminster stations could be damaged without the plan, under which groundwater is pumped out every year.

London Underground pumps 14 million litres of water from its network each year to cope with flooding. According to the Environment Agency, which has been monitoring London's groundwater since 1991, groundwater levels are rising at about 3 metres per year compared with 2.5 metres in the early 1990s. In some areas, groundwater in the London Basin (the area underlying the whole of London, stretching from the North Downs to the Chilterns) is only 40 metres from the surface.

A number of other problems in London relate to groundwater (Figure 13.3).

Water quality in the River Thames has improved dramatically in recent decades. In the nineteenth and early twentieth centuries, water quality declined as industrial and population growth led to large volumes of effluent being emptied into the river. Sewage treatment plants in the twentieth century and the decline in manufacturing have led to an improvement in water quality. By 1974 the first salmon for nearly 150 years was caught in the River Thames and in 1997 a freshwater crab was taken from the river.

- Flows in several rivers have been depleted as a result of large groundwater abstractions close to the headwaters or along the river valleys. Worst affected are the rivers Misbourne, Ver, Wey, Pang and the Letcombe Brook.

- Abstraction near the Thames estuary has resulted in saline intrusion into groundwater several kilometres inland along the River Thames.

- Most sites which have been considered suitable for waste disposal and landfill are quarries located on aquifers, such as sand and gravel quarries overlying the chalk aquifer, as in south Hertfordshire – the waste could pollute drinking water.

- There is continued pressure for redevelopment of former industrial sites, many of which occupy prime locations in urban areas. The land is frequently contaminated and there is often associated groundwater pollution, with potential for pollution remaining.

- Rising nitrate concentrations are evident in the groundwater.

- Chemicals, such as pesticides, are in widespread usage across the catchment of the River Thames and the frequency of detection in groundwater has risen.

- Groundwater in some urban areas has been contaminated by leakage from sewers, and through widespread usage of chemicals such as solvents.

Figure 13.3 *Groundwater problems in the Lower Thames Basin*
Source: adapted from Nagle, G. and Spencer, K., 1997, Sustainable development, Hodder and Stoughton

Contaminated land

The area around the River Thames in east London has been described as the area where London 'generates its energy and dumps its waste'. The result of this is that much of the land is contaminated. One such area is the Barking Levels. Here the soil and air is contaminated and the marshes have been used as a dumping ground for industrial waste – and murder victims. One part of the Levels has been used as a landfill site since Victorian times and there are nearly 6 metres of compressed rubbish.

In places, the land has been contaminated with radon gas, asbestos, fuel ash, lead and cyanide. The Hart's Lane Estate by Barking Creek, for example, was built on an old asbestos works and is now suffering from contaminated air. In the nearby Black Lagoon, levels of lead are as high as 33 000 ppm (parts per million) in the soil. In addition, gases given off by the old gas works and former industries (from chemical reactions building up over a period of time under pressure) have been known to ignite spontaneously.

QUESTIONS

1 Explain why the quality of London's water has improved in recent years.

2 Why are groundwater levels in London rising?

3 Briefly explain how groundwater can become contaminated.

4 What is meant by the term 'contaminated land'? Describe the hazards associated with contaminated land.

MEXICO CITY

Like London, Mexico City experiences many hazards (Figure 13.4). These include poor air quality, earthquakes and shortages of water. In addition, there are hazards related to industrial accidents, poverty and infectious diseases. Mexico City has a population density which exceeds 14 000 people per square kilometre in some areas. This intensifies the risk of hazards. For example, on 19 November 1984 over 450 people were killed when a gas truck exploded in a liquefied gas storage depot in San Junico suburb. Fires covered an area of just 20 blocks but more than 4350 people were severely burned in the incident. Over 30 000 were made homeless and 300 000 people had to be evacuated.

Figure 13.4 *Environmental hazards in Mexico City: destruction from the 1985 Mexico earthquake*

Environmental problems are rife in Mexico City. The concentration of 3.5 million vehicles and 40 000 factories emits 12 000 tons of gaseous waste daily. Smog reduces visibility daily to about two kilometres. The city has the world's highest ozone concentration and one of the highest figures for carbon monoxide. In 1994 air quality was acceptable (WHO levels of acceptability) on only 20 days in the year! In addition, there is very little green space in the city.

There is a serious problem caused by the dumping of hazardous waste – there are no legal landfill sites and only five recycling plants in Mexico City. Illegal dumping at Rincon Verde has led to increased risk of diseases in the area, underground fires and pollution of the water table.

Air quality

Mexico City's 20 million inhabitants suffer some of the worst air quality in the world. The city is located in a basin surrounded by mountains, so air becomes trapped in the basin by the surrounding high ground; in winter cold air from the surrounding hills sinks, producing frequent temperature inversions. Smogs are common between November and May. In 1992 poor air quality (as defined by the WHO), damaging to health, occurred on 192 days, over half of the year. Smogs can be so severe that schools are closed for a month at a time, and industries have to reduce production by up to 75%. It is thought that about 3000 deaths annually are caused by the smogs.

Mexico City has very poor air quality for a number of reasons:

- a location in a high altitude basin
- the latitude (19° North) and altitude (2250 metres) produce winter sunshine which allows the formation of photochemical smogs
- urban heat island, which can draw pollutants into the city centre
- frequent temperature inversions in the winter which trap pollutants at low levels
- a large population size – 20 million people
- the continual migration of people to the city increases the emissions of pollutants
- because the city is prone to earthquakes, people use portable gas cylinders rather than piped gas; leaking gas adds benzene
- the large number of industries, of all kinds – including large/small scale, heavy/mixed/light, old, inefficient and unregulated/modern, chemical – over 35 000 in total
- 3.5 million cars
- because Mexico City is so vast, people travel long distances to work by car, adding to the volume of pollutants in the atmosphere
- transport accounts for up to 97% of carbon monoxide, 66% of nitrogen dioxide and 54% of VOCs – most cars are old, inefficient and not strictly regulated.

The city has high levels of carbon monoxide, ozone, lead, PM_{10}s and sulphur dioxide (Figure 13.5 on page 120). In 1992, acceptable levels of ozone, PM_{10}s and carbon monoxide (as defined by WHO) occurred on only eight days! In 1994 it was not much better – air quality was acceptable on just 11 days out of the whole year.

In Mexico City, levels of ozone are especially high in the

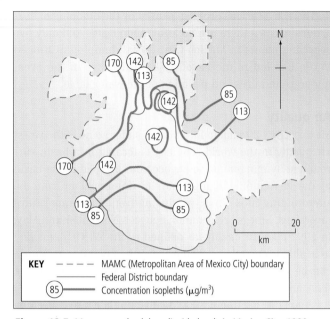

Figure 13.5 *Mean annual sulphur dioxide levels in Mexico City, 1989. The WHO guideline is 40-60 µg/m³*
Source: Middleton, N., 1995, Global casino, Edward Arnold

south-west. During the day, air flows are frequently from the north-east towards the residential areas in the south and west; by the time the air reaches the south-west, photochemical reactions have taken place, producing very high levels of ozone and petrochemical smog.

Industry in Mexico City, including oil companies, metal foundries, cement and paper manufacturers, are concentrated in the north of the city. Here lead concentrations are high; the prevailing air flows transport the pollution problem to the residential areas in the south and west.

Up to 2 million people, one tenth of the population, suffer diseases caused by air pollution. It is thought that the health costs related to ozone are US$100 million a year – and PM_{10}s US$800 million a year! The particulate problem is exacerbated by dust from the dried bed of Lake Texcoco to the north-east of the city, the large landfill sites surrounding Mexico City and the urban heating systems.

There have been a number of schemes to reduce air pollution in Mexico City. In 1989 the authorities introduced colour-coded permits, allowing access to the city on specified days, to restrict traffic in the city. The scheme has reduced the number of vehicles in the city by up to 400 000 a day and has improved air quality by as much as 15%. Drivers face fines of US$600 if they break the restriction. In addition, all taxis over 10 years old have been replaced and the amount of lead in petrol has been halved. Nevertheless, these schemes are limited by the amount of money available to the government and to individuals. Mexico's foreign debt and the poverty experienced by many people means that a number of more costly policies to improve the environment cannot be implemented.

Water

At an urban scale, water shortages in Mexico City are acute. Although Mexico City is renowned for its smog, there is another major hazard. Residents claim that if they don't die from air pollution they will die either from thirst or from drowning in their own sewage.

The main source of water for Mexico City's 20 million people is an aquifer below the city. However, the aquifer is running dry. As a result, Mexico City is sinking at a rate of 50 centimetres a decade. Dangerous cracks in the clay sediments threaten to contaminate the aquifer, which lies just 100 metres below the surface.

Mexico City uses 62 cubic metres of water a second. Two-thirds comes from the aquifer. The rest, 19 tonnes per second, is pumped from dams 120 kilometres away. The electricity needed to pump the water would support a medium-sized town for a day.

Mexico City's demand for water has brought it into conflict with neighbouring states. As the city uses more water there is less available for irrigation. In addition, up to 30% of Mexico City's water is lost through leakages and theft. Two solutions have been proposed:
- metering the use of water
- charging residents for the use of water.

Either measure is likely to be very unpopular and so far the government has resisted moves by planners and environmentalists to introduce meters.

Earthquakes

The epicentre of the 1985 earthquake was 370 kilometres away from Mexico City (Figure 13.6). Although there was some damage along the Pacific Coast, most of the damage was in Mexico City. There, over 7000 people died, 40 000 people were injured, and 30 000 were made homeless. In one building, Nuevo Leon, almost everyone from 200 families was killed. The General Hospital collapsed, burying 600 staff and patients. The economic cost was estimated at over US$4 billion. A number of places close to the epicentre were affected. However, none were as badly affected as Mexico City, in particular the buildings on the vulnerable former lake beds.

The worst consequences of the earthquake were concentrated in a very small area within Mexico City. Fewer than 4% of buildings in Mexico City's core were destroyed. The key factors appear to be unstable sediments, high housing densities and poor building structures. Buildings on 'susceptible' soils and alluvial (river) deposits are prone to collapse. For example, in the 1957 earthquake in Mexico City, 96% of the houses damaged were built on the Lake Texcoco sediments. Similarly, most of the damage in the 1985 earthquake was on susceptible sediments on the floor of an old lake bed. When shaken in an earthquake, the foundations of structures in these sediments break up, lose strength, or become waterlogged.

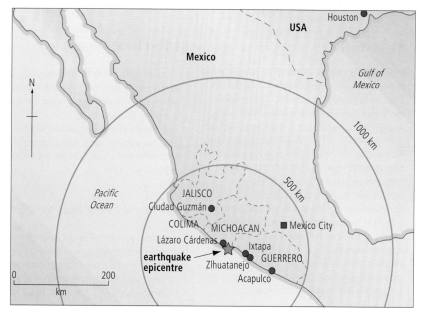

Figure 13.6 *The epicentre of the 1985 Mexico earthquake*
Source: Hewitt, K., 1997, Regions of risk, Longman

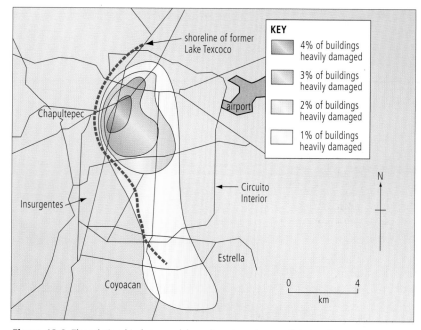

Figure 13.8 *The relationship between lake sediments and areas of destruction*
Source: Hewitt, K., 1997, Regions of risk, Longman

Figure 13.7 shows the relationship between the percentage of buildings damaged and the unstable sediments of the old lake bed. The thicker the lake sediments, the greater the number of buildings damaged (Figure 13.8). Many of the victims were relative newcomers forced to live in unsafe areas in poorly constructed buildings.

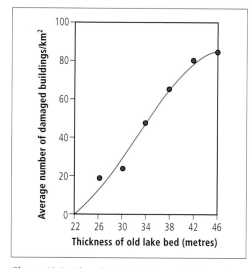

Figure 13.7 *The relationship between thickness of lake sediment and numbers of buildings damaged*
Source: Hewitt, K., 1997, Regions of risk, Longman

QUESTIONS

1 Why is Mexico City prone to earthquakes?

2 Describe the relationship between **(i)** the distribution of lake sediments and the impact of the earthquake (Figure 13.7), and **(ii)** the thickness of lake sediments and the damage caused (Figure 13.8).

SUMMARY

In this chapter we have examined the hazards in two of the world's great cities, London and Mexico City. There are many contrasts. London is a developed world city which has deindustrialised; Mexico City is in a developing country and is much larger. Migration continues in Mexico City, whereas London has been experiencing counterurbanisation for many years. We have seen that there are many contrasts between the hazards experienced in each city. Mexico City is prone to earthquakes and its residents live in low quality, high density housing. By contrast, flooding is a threat in London. However, there are similarities, notably air pollution, industrial hazards and contaminated land. The ways in which the residents and the authorities in each city cope with the problems depend, in part, on the resources available to them and also on population pressures.

QUESTIONS

1 Compare and contrast the environmental hazards experienced in large cities in the developed world with those in the developing world. Use examples to support your answer.
2 With the use of examples, explain why London and Londoners are better able to cope with environmental hazards than the authorities and residents of Mexico City.

Extended (Project) work

Find out from your local City or County Engineering Department if there are any environmental hazards in your area. What has been done to manage the threat they pose? For example, are there any:
- building restrictions
- land-use management plans
- public notices and/or restricted access?

Visit your local library and use the local press to see what hazards may have been reported.

BIBLIOGRAPHY AND RECOMMENDED READING

Elsom, D., 1996, *Smog alert: managing urban air quality*, Earthscan
Hewitt, K., 1997, *Regions of risk*, Longman
HMSO, 1997, *Focus on London*, HMSO
Nagle, G., 1998, *Changing settlements*, Nelson
Pick, J. and Butler, E., 1994, *The Mexico handbook: economic and demographic maps and statistics*, Westview Press
Ward, P., 1991, *Mexico City*, Wiley

WEB SITE

Westminster City Council: air quality home page –
http://www.wcceh.gov.uk/

Abbreviations

CFC	-	chlorofluorocarbon
CO	-	carbon monoxide
CO_2	-	carbon dioxide
HCFC	-	hydrochlorofluorocarbons
ELDC	-	economically less developed countries
EMDCs	-	economically more developed countries
GNP	-	gross national product
HCl	-	hydrogen chloride
NO	-	nitric oxide
NO_2	-	nitrogen dioxide
NOx	-	nitrogen oxides
O_3	-	ozone
$PM_{10}s$	-	particulates
SO_2	-	sulphur dioxide
VOC	-	volatile organic compounds

Glossary

Active volcano   A volcano that has erupted within recorded history.

Aerosols   Extremely fine particles or droplets that are carried in suspension; volcanic aerosols result from the reaction of volcanic gases with water vapour in the atmosphere.

Aftershock   An earthquake that occurs shortly after a major quake.

Bankfull discharge   The discharge measured when a river is at bankfull stage.

Beaufort Scale   A scale used for measuring and recording wind velocity.

Behavioural school of thought   Behaviouralists argue that people who live in hazardous areas are aware of the dangers but have decided to live there because the advantages outweigh the disadvantages.

Chemical weathering   The decomposition of rocks and minerals as chemical reactions transform them into new chemical combinations that are stable at or near the earthís surface.

Contaminants   Materials that have harmful impacts and degrade the environment.

Constructive boundary   A plate boundary where new material is formed as plates move apart, e.g. the Mid-Atlantic Ridge. It is also known as a divergent margin, or spreading ridges.

Core   The spherical mass, largely metallic iron, at the centre of the earth.

Coriolis effect   An effect which causes any body that moves freely with respect to the rotating earth (e.g. winds) to veer to the right in the Northern Hemisphere and to the left in the Southern Hemisphere.

Crust   The outermost and thinnest of the earthís compositional layers, which consists of rocky matter that is less dense than the rocks of the mantle below.

Cyclone   An atmospheric low-pressure system that gives rise to roughly circular, inward-spiralling wind motion.

Depression   An area of low pressure, also known as a cyclone or low pressure system.

Desert   Area where annual rainfall is consistently less than 250 millimetres or in which the rate of evaporation consistently exceeds the rate of precipitation.

Desertification   The spread of desert into non-desert areas.

Destructive boundary   A zone where a tectonic plate is destroyed, for example, the destruction of the Nazca plate (oceanic) as it is pushed beneath the South America (continental) plate. It is also known as a convergent or subduction margin.

Disaster   A hazard which has resulted in human death and/or the destruction of property.

Discharge   The quantity of water that passes a given point on the bank of a river within a given period of time.

Dormant volcano   A volcano that has not erupted in recent memory and shows no signs of current activity, but is not deeply eroded.

Drainage basin   The total area that contributes water to a river. It is also known as the catchment.

Drought   An extended period of time with exceptionally low precipitation.

Earthquake   A sudden movement of the earthís surface.

El Nino   A warming of surface waters in the eastern equatorial Pacific Ocean.

Epicentre   The point on the earthís surface directly above the focus of an earthquake.

Extinct volcano   A volcano that has not erupted within recorded history, is deeply eroded, and shows no signs of future activity.

Flash flood   A flood in which the lag time is exceptionally short, i.e. hours or minutes.

Flood   A discharge great enough to cause a body of water to overflow its channel and submerge surrounding land.

Flood-frequency curve   The curve produced on a graph when floods of the same magnitude at a given location are plotted with respect to their recurrence interval.

Floodplain   The part of any stream valley that is regularly inundated during floods.

Flow   A mass movement that involves the movement of mixtures of sediment and water.

Focus   The area where energy which causes an earthquake is first released.

Frost heave   The lifting of soil by the freezing of water in it.

Gale   A low pressure system with wind speeds of between 51 and 101 kilometres/hour.

Greenhouse effect   The trapping or reflection by the earthís atmosphere of long-wavelength heat rays from the earthís surface.

Ground-level ozone   Ozone that occurs in the lower part of the atmosphere; tropospheric ozone. Groundwater The water contained in spaces within bedrock and regolith. (Regolith is the loose material, for example soil and sediments, overlying the bedrock.)

Gulleys   Distinct, narrow stream channels that result from rapid downward water erosion.

Hazard   An event which poses a threat to human life and property.

Hazard assessment   The process of determining when and where hazards have occurred, the severity of the effects, the frequency of events, and the likely impact if it were to occur again.

High-level ozone   A form of oxygen, consisting of three atoms, which helps to control the temperature of the atmosphere and the amount of ultraviolet radiation reaching the earthís surface.

Human hazards   Human-generated hazards that arise from pollution and degradation of the natural environment, e.g. contamination of surface and underground water, depletion of the ozone layer, global climatic warming.

Hurricane   A tropical cyclonic storm with winds that exceed 120 kilometre/hour.

Hydrograph   A graph in which river discharge is plotted against time.

Infiltration   The process by which water from precipitation soaks into the soil.

Jokulhlaup   A large and sudden burst of glacier meltwater caused by volcanic activity and the build up of pressure beneath a glacier.

Lag time   The time between the start of precipitation and the peak flood.

Lahar   A volcanic mudflow.

Landslide   Any perceptible downslope movement of bedrock, regolith, or a mixture of both.

Lateral blast   A sideways volcanic eruption of pulverised rock and hot gases.

Lava   Magma that reaches the earthís surface through a volcanic vent and pours out over the landscape.

Liquefaction   The rapid fluidisation of sediment as the result of a disturbance or an abrupt shock, such as an earthquake.

Load   The particles of sediment and dissolved matter that are carried along by a river.

Magma   Molten rock, sometimes containing suspended mineral grains and dissolved gases, that forms when temperatures rise sufficiently for melting to occur in the earthís crust or mantle.

Mantle   The thick shell of dense, rocky matter that surrounds the earth's core.

Mass movement   The movement of materials downslope as a result of the pull of gravity.

Modified Mercalli Intensity Scale   A scale used to compare earthquakes based on the amount of vibration people feel during low-magnitude quakes and the extent of damage to buildings during high-magnitude quakes.

Natural hazards   The wide range of natural circumstances, materials, processes and events that are hazardous to humans, such as locust infestations, wildfires, or tornadoes, in addition to strictly geological hazards.

Overland run-off   The portion of precipitation that flows over the surface of the land.

P-waves   Primary, or compressional, earthquake waves, which move fast, through solids or liquids.

Particulates   Pollutants that are carried in suspension in the air as extremely fine, solid particles.

Peak discharge   The point at which the maximum discharge for a particular flood is reached.

PM$_{10}$s   Tiny particulates which can penetrate the lungs

Pollution   Materials with harmful impacts on the natural environment; the act of releasing such materials.

Pyroclast   A fragment of rock ejected during a volcanic eruption.

Pyroclastic flow   A hot, highly mobile flow of tephra that rushes down the side of a volcano during a major eruption.

Recurrence interval   The average interval between occurrences of two events, such as floods of equal magnitude.

Richter scale   A scale based on the recorded amplitudes of seismic body waves for comparing the amounts of energy released by earthquakes.

Risk assessment   The process of establishing the probability that a hazardous event of a particular magnitude will occur within a given period and estimating its impact, taking into account the locations of buildings, facilities, and emergency systems in the community, the potential exposure to the physical effects of the hazardous situation or event, and the community's vulnerability when subjected to those physical effects.

S-waves   Secondary, or shear, earthquake waves, which are slower moving, and can only move through solids.

Safety factor   The ratio of shear strength to shear stress, which determines the tendency of a slope to fail.

Saffir-Simpson scale   Classification of hurricanes based upon wind speed, damage caused, and accompanying storm surge.

Secondary hazard   A hazard that occurs after the main event, for example a fire following an earthquake, or a famine following a flood.

Seismic belts   Large tracts of the earth's surface that are subject to frequent earthquakes.

Seismic gaps   Places along a fault where earthquakes have not occurred for a long time even though tectonic stresses are still active and elastic energy is steadily building up.

Seismic waves   Elastic disturbances that spread out in all directions from an earthquake's point of origin. (Elastic can be used to refer to any substance that returns to its original shape is the stress does not exceed its elastic character.)

Shear strength   The internal resistance of a body to movement.

Shear stress   The force acting on a body that causes movement of the body downslope.

Sheet wash   Erosion by water through overland flow during heavy rains.

Slide   The rapid displacement of rock or sediment in one direction, with no rotation.

Slump   A type of slope failure involving the downward and outward movement of rock or regolith along a concave surface.

Smog   A yellowish-brownish haze that results when airborne contaminants interact with sunlight and undergo a variety of complex photochemical reactions.

Solifluction   The slow movement of rock debris, saturated with water, and not confined to definite channels, down a slope under the force of gravity.

Storm   An intense low pressure system. On the Beaufort Scale, storms have a wind speed of between 102 and 120 kilometres/hour.

Storm surge   An abnormal, temporary rise in water levels in oceans or lakes due to low atmospheric pressure associated with storms.

Structuralist school of thought   Structuralists believe that people are constrained by society and/or politics, and do not have freedom of choice, and that P some people have to live in hazardous areas because they are too poor to afford safer conditions.

Subsidence   The sinking or collapse of a portion of the land surface.

Technological hazards   Hazards associated with everyday exposure to hazardous substances, such as radon, mercury, asbestos or coal dust, usually through some aspect of the use of these substances in our built environment.

Tephra   A loose assemblage of pyroclasts.

Tornado   A cyclonic storm with a very intense low-pressure centre, generally found over continental interiors.

Tsunami   A very long wavelength ocean wave that is generated by a sudden displacement of the sea floor.

Typhoon   A term used to describe a tropical cyclonic storm that originates in the western Pacific Ocean.

Volcano   The vent from which magma, solid rock debris and gases erupt.

Weather   The state of the atmosphere at a given time and place.

Index